Exploring the Great Lakes

A Logbook of Adventures

by Patricia Westfield & Nan Soper

River Road Publications, Inc.

ISBN: 0-938682-73-3

Produced by River Road Publications, Inc., Spring Lake, Michigan 49456
Printed in the United States of America

Cover art by Tony Boisvert.

CD-ROM produced by Vince Deur Productions, LLC.

Exploring the Great Lakes: A Logbook of Adventures

 THIS SYMBOL INDICATES TOPICS THAT CORRESPOND TO THE EXPLORING THE GREAT LAKES CD-ROM. IT CONTAINS MORE THAN 30 MINUTES OF FOOTAGE FROM AROUND THE GREAT LAKES, LISTENING ACTIVITIES, QUOTES, STORIES, POEMS, AND OTHER INFORMATION.

Exploring the Great Lakes

Hi, I'm Alex. My parents are teachers. We spend weeks on the Great Lakes every summer in our sailboat, the Blue Heron. I've been keeping journals of our trips as long as I can remember. I was so little when I started that I have one journal with nothing but pictures I made of the sun, waves, and little squiggles that I think were supposed to be seagulls. Some parts of the journals just talk about the weather and what we ate for dinner. They are sooo b-o-r-i-n-g. But some of the entries are pretty interesting and I'm glad I saved them. My mom and dad helped me use the best pages of the journals to make this book. I hope you like it. Have fun exploring the Great Lakes!

P.S. Start your own journal today. If you have a boring day, write about how boring it was!
Or take a hint from my friend Skippy and write about one of his ideas.

Hey! I dare you to try to answer these. I bet you won't know all of them!

1. How many thirsty people drink Great Lakes water in one day?
   A) 25 thousand   B) 250 thousand   C) 25 million

2. Which famous Great Lakes shipwreck had a song written about it?
   A) the *Titanic*   B) the Unsinkable Molly Brown   C) the *Edmund Fitzgerald*

3. What does the acronym HOMES stand for?
   A) How Our Moms Eat Shellfish   B) Help Our Marine Environment Survive
   C) Huron, Ontario, Michigan, Erie, Superior—the five Great Lakes

4. What is said to "never give up its dead"?
   A) The ship's cat when it catches a mouse.   B) Sand dunes, which shift to bury and swallow up houses.
   C) Lake Superior, which is so cold that bodies don't decompose and float to the surface.

5. What is the Great Lakes Triangle?
   A) An area where an unusually high number of shipwrecks have occured.   B) A major population area formed by Chicago, Detroit, and Traverse City.   C) The interaction of sand, wind, & water.

6. About how many gallons of water does the average person in the U.S. use each day?
   A) 20-30 gallons   B) 54-59 gallons   C) 80-100 gallons

This is Skippy.
What do you think
I look like? Draw a
picture of me.

MAP ACTIVITY
On your Great Lakes Activity Map label the five Great Lakes. Label the eight states and the two Canadian provinces that border the Great Lakes and the St. Lawrence River.

WHAT WOULD BE THE WORST PART OF LIVING ON A BOAT FOR THE SUMMER? WHAT WOULD BE BEST?

Our Place in Time

I was skipping stones on Lake Michigan last night and found a petoskey stone. Today we went into the town of Petoskey, Michigan, where I bought a kit to polish my stone. The lady in the shop said the town was named for the stones because they are so common here. She also said most of the stones have been picked up for souvenirs and I was lucky to find one. They are really fossils of the coral reefs which were here when the salt water seas covered the area 500 million years ago. That's a long time ago—it's hard to imagine.

TAPE TIMELINE
Use masking or duct tape to make a 30-foot line on the floor or wall. Each foot represents 100 million years. Make a sign for each time period which includes information from the chart. Set your signs up along the timeline or have friends stand along the timeline holding the signs. They can be "Time Guides" and explain each time period as people walk by.

PAPER TIMELINE
Use a roll of paper to make a 30-foot timeline on the wall. Each foot represents 100 million years. Mark and label the time periods on the timeline. Draw pictures on the timeline to represent the life, resources, and events during each time period.

TIME PERIOD	LOCATION ON TIMELINE	EVENTS IN THE REGION	LIFE IN THE REGION	RESOURCES FORMING
Precambrian Era	3.5 billion years ago (0 feet)	Volcanic activity builds land and mountains	algae, fungi, bacteria	iron, gold, copper
Paleozoic Era	600-280 million years ago (24 feet)	Saltwater seas exist here	sea creatures & plants, insects, reptiles, tree ferns	salt, limestone, coal
Mesozoic Era	230-135 million years ago (27 feet 8 inches)	Remains of plants & animals accumulate	dinosaurs, birds, mammals, plants	oil
Cenozoic Era	70 million years-present (29 feet 9.5 inches)	Ancient river valleys exist	man	
Ice Age	2 million years ago (29 feet 11.75 inches)	Glaciers cover area gouging and compressing the land	mastadons, mammoths, grasslands, forests	
Present Day	10,000 years ago (29 feet 11.84 inches)	Melting glaciers fill the lakes	Native Americans	water, gravel, sand, soil

1. What was the longest era?
2. During what era were petoskey stones formed?
3. Some of the mountainous areas in the north were made by _____.
4. Use descriptive words to compare the age of the Great Lakes to the age of the earth.
5. What appeared during the time of the ancient river valleys?
6. What <u>types</u> of resources were formed first?

Before the Ice Age

I was looking at a map of the Great Lakes and thinking about how strange they are. How did huge lakes end up in the middle of a continent, and why do they connect?

Long before the Ice Age, about 70 million years ago, the Great Lakes region was a flat land high above the ocean (a plateau). Rivers cut deep valleys in the plateau. Scientists think some of the valleys were as much as 1,000 feet deep. Compare the two maps below to answer the questions. You may also follow the directions to make a map with an overlay comparing the modern lakes to the ancient rivers.

1. Match the ancient river or rivers to the present body of water which is in the same area.

  <u>Ancient Rivers</u>   <u>Current Bodies of Water and Waterways</u>

A. Laurentian River   _____Lake Michigan   _____Georgian Bay

B. Erigan River   _____Lake Huron   _____Lake Ontario

C. Huronian River   _____St. Lawrence Seaway   _____Saginaw Bay

                                                         _____Lake Erie

2. Make a hypothesis (a guess based on what you know) explaining why the Great Lakes are in about the same place as the ancient river valleys. Write your answer in the space below.

ACTIVITY: MAKE A MAP WITH OVERLAY

Cut out the maps along the solid lines. Place the Great Lakes Map on top of the Ancient Rivers Map and tape or staple them together on the edge with the dotted line.

WRITE A STORY WHICH TAKES PLACE DURING THE ICE AGE.

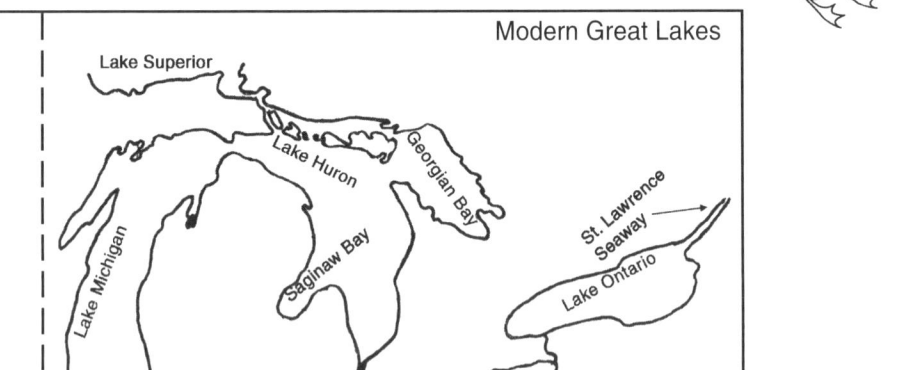

Ancient Rivers

Laurentian R. — Laurentian R. — Laurentian River — Huronian River — Erigan River

Modern Great Lakes

Lake Superior — Lake Huron — Georgian Bay — Lake Michigan — Saginaw Bay — St. Lawrence Seaway — Lake Ontario — Lake Erie

Building the Great Lakes

On Kelleys Island I saw rocks with huge grooves cut right into them. It looked like a giant had taken the fingers of one hand and dragged them along the rock, gouging out deep parallel grooves. But it was the glaciers that dug the grooves in the rock as they moved across it. I wish I could have seen the glaciers. They must have been incredibly huge and powerful.

During the Ice Age gigantic sheets of ice called glaciers formed near the North Pole. The glaciers slid slowly south across what is now Canada. Finally they slid down into the Great Lakes region.

The glaciers changed the land. Their great weight compressed the surface of the earth. They gouged out the ancient river valleys, making them much wider and deeper. The valleys became huge bowls, or basins.

The glaciers also picked up and carried sand, gravel, and boulders with them. As the glaciers melted, this debris was left behind. It lined the edges of the basins and it blocked the mouths of the rivers so the water was trapped. When the giant glaciers melted, their waters filled the basins. The Great Lakes were born!

1. What was here before the Great Lakes existed?

2. What part of the world did the glaciers come from?

3. Explain three ways that glaciers changed the land.

4. How were the shapes of the river valleys changed?

5. What happened to the mouths of the rivers?

6. Where did much of the water in the Lakes come from?

MAP ACTIVITY

Label Kelleys Island on your Great Lakes Activity Map (13J). Which Great Lake is it in?

EXPERIMENT: HOW DO GLACIERS CHANGE THE LAND?

It's hard to imagine how frozen water could reshape the land and create the Great Lakes. This experiment will help you understand the power of ice.

Find a plastic or cardboard container such as a juice or whipped topping container. Fill it with a mixture of water, sand, and gravel and put it in the freezer. When the mixture is frozen solid remove the ice block from the container. Take your "glacier" outside to a small hill with soft soil and loose pebbles. Place your "glacier" near the top of the hill and push down on it while moving it down the hill. Push down hard–remember the glaciers weighed many many tons. After you have moved the ice block part way down the hill mark your starting and stopping points with sticks or pencils. Then leave the ice block where it is and do something else for a while until the ice melts. Then examine the area.

What does your "glacier trail" look like? What is left behind where the glacier melted? Look around: if a glacier passed through tomorrow, how do you think your area would change?

EXPERIMENT: HOW DO GLACIERS MOVE?

Fill a square cake pan with water and freeze it. Remove the ice block from the pan. Place it on a wire rack in the freezer. Put a brick or similiar object on top of the ice block. After 24 hours check the bottom of the ice block. What happened?

The bottom of a glacier has a lot of pressure on it from the immense weight of the glacier. This pressure makes the bottom of the glacier melt into a thick fluid. This fluid flows out from the glacier and refreezes, allowing the glacier to slide on land. Some glaciers move a few inches while others may move many yards in a day.

The Sweetwater Seas

From out here on Lake Michigan I can see nothing but water in every direction. It's like being on the ocean instead of a lake. The French explorers called the Great Lakes "Sweetwater Seas." I can see why. They really are as big as a sea, only not salty. I looked them up in a book and found out that the Great Lakes hold 65,000 trillion gallons of water—that's 1/5 of the earth's fresh water!

Lake	Volume	Surface Area	Greatest Depth
Huron	850 cubic miles	23,000 square miles	750 feet
Ontario	393 cubic miles	7,550 square miles	802 feet
Erie	116 cubic miles	9,910 square miles	210 feet
Superior	2,900 cubic miles	31,820 square miles	1,330 feet
Michigan	1,180 cubic miles	22,300 square miles	923 feet

1. Which lake is the "greatest" of the Great Lakes because it has the greatest surface area, volume, and depth of all the lakes?

2. Lake Ontario holds much more water than Lake Erie even though it has a smaller surface area. Explain how this is possible.

3. How many Lake Eries would need to be stacked up to be almost as deep as Lake Superior?

4. Look at the shapes of lakes Michigan and Huron and at the information in the chart. Explain why some people call lakes Michigan and Huron "Siamese twins."

5. Why is it important to keep the "Sweetwater Seas" clean?

6. Find and label Lake St. Clair on your Activity Map. It is between lakes Huron and Erie. Notice its location and size. Some people think it should be called a Great Lake. What do you think?

GREAT NAMES

Over the centuries the names of the lakes have changed many times. At one time the French misunderstood the Indian name for Lake Michigan and called it the "lake of the stinking people"! Today the names of three of the Great Lakes come from Native American words. Lake Michigan was "michigami," or big water, to the Ojibwa. Lake Erie gets its name from the Iroquois word for wildcat. Lake Ontario was named "beautiful water" by the Iroquois. Lake Huron was named by the French after the Huron Indians, and Lake Superior was named by French explorers "le lac superieur," meaning that it was the "highest lake" of the chain of lakes.

IF YOU COULD RENAME ALL FIVE OF THE GREAT LAKES, WHAT WOULD YOU NAME EACH ONE? WHY?

Where Does the Water Go?

Today we saw the St. Marys River, which connects Lake Superior to Lakes Michigan and Huron. The water goes really fast down the river because the elevation drops a lot. It would be fun to canoe if it wasn't so rocky. I wonder where the water goes from here?

GOING WITH THE FLOW

Have you ever made a little lake out of the mashed potatoes on your plate and filled it with gravy? What happens when you take a forkfull of potatoes out of the side of your "potato lake"? The gravy runs out of the lake and on to your plate, right? That's because liquids always flow from higher levels (elevations) to lower elevations. The Great Lakes are at various elevations, so the water in them flows from the highest lake to the lowest lake just like the gravy runs out of your potato lake. Use the diagram to answer the questions.

1. How many feet does the water drop between Lake Superior and the Atlantic Ocean?

2. Between which two Great Lakes does the water drop the most?

3. This change in elevation creates what tourist attraction?

4. If the Great Lakes are connected to the ocean, then why aren't the Great Lakes salty?

LESS THAN ONE PERCENT OF THE WATER IN THE GREAT LAKES FLOWS OUT INTO THE OCEAN EACH YEAR.

5. If someone poured a toxic chemical into Lake St. Clair, which rivers and bodies of water would be contaminated?

RETENTION TIMES OF THE LAKES

If you put a drop of oil in one of the Great Lakes it would first circulate in the lake for a while before flowing out. This period of time that liquids remain in the lake is called the retention time of the lake. It is based on the volume of water in the lake and the rate at which water flows out of the lake. Use the chart to decide if each statement is true or false. Circle T for true or F for false.

T F 6. The greater the volume of a lake the longer it takes for water to circulate out of it.
T F 7. It would take over 300 years for a toxic chemical to flow out of the Great Lakes.
T F 8. Lake Ontario has the shortest retention time because it has the smallest volume.

Lake	Volume (cubic miles)	Retention (years)
Erie	116	2.6
Huron	850	22
Michigan	1,180	99
Ontario	393	6
Superior	2,900	191

MAP ACTIVITY
- Label the connecting waterways on your Great Lakes Activity Map.
- Write in the elevation above sea level under the name of each Great Lake.
- Draw a few small blue arrows on the map to show the direction the water flows through the Great Lakes and out to the ocean. Add the water flow arrows to your map's legend.

The Ever-Changing Great Lakes

My dad drives me crazy. He says we better go see Niagara Falls this summer before it dries up! He says the water in the lakes is going to start flowing the opposite way so it won't go down the falls anymore! He is always making up ridiculous stories to see if I'll believe them. My mom says he is telling the truth, but I still don't believe it.

At the end of the Ice Age, the glaciers began to melt along their southern edge. The land that had been compressed by their weight began to rebound, or rise back up. Since the southwest part of the region was the first to be free of the weight of the glaciers it was first to rebound. The rebounding of the land as the glaciers melted from the southwest toward the northeast caused the whole region to be tilted. It is now like a gigantic hillside with Lake Michigan near the top. The water in the lakes flows down the tilt and out the St. Lawrence River into the Atlantic Ocean.

But that's not the end of the story. Land in the northeast is still rebounding. When that area stops rising it will be the highest part of the region and Lake Michigan will be at the bottom. The slope of the land will be reversed.

What will happen to the flow of the lake waters? You got it! They will be reversed. Scientists estimate that by the year 3500 all the lake waters except Lake Ontario will flow down into Lake Michigan and through the Illinois Waterway to the Mississippi River and the Gulf of Mexico.

TILT IT! TRY IT!

Hold your Great Lakes Activity Map parallel to the floor. Raise the southwest corner of the map up a few inches. This represents the overall tilt of the region as it is now. Which way would the water flow through the lakes? Now raise the northeast corner of the map up a few inches higher than the southwest corner. This represents the overall tilt of the region after the land has finished rebounding. Which way would the water flow now? Our map is flat so it does not account for differing land elevations and features like Niagara Falls, but you can still see the general effect of the rebounding of the land.

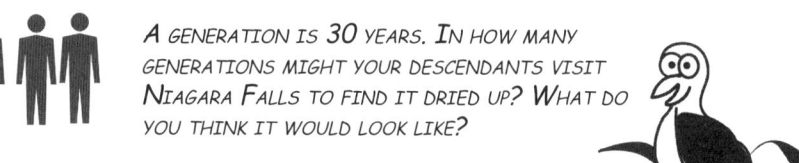

A GENERATION IS 30 YEARS. IN HOW MANY GENERATIONS MIGHT YOUR DESCENDANTS VISIT NIAGARA FALLS TO FIND IT DRIED UP? WHAT DO YOU THINK IT WOULD LOOK LIKE?

I PREDICT THAT IN 3500...

Scientists use facts along with observations to predict how the earth might change in the future. Look at the Great Lakes Activity Map and use what you know, and your imagination, to predict how the Lakes might change when the flow is reversed.

1. What will happen to Niagara Falls?

2. What will the waters from Lake Ontario flow into? Why?

3. How might the size and shape of Lake Michigan change?

4. What might happen to the St. Lawrence Seaway?

5. How might the Illinois and Mississippi Rivers change?

MAP ACTIVITY

Label the Illinois Waterway (7L through 8K) and Mississippi River (1C through 5L) on your Great Lakes Activity Map.

Water Wave Science

It was such a nice day that we decided to drift, swim, and nap. I wonder why the Blue Heron isn't washed ashore by the waves?

WHAT IS A WAVE?   You probably know about sound and light waves. Another type of wave is a water wave. All waves, including sound, light, and water waves, are simply energy traveling from one place to another through a medium, like air or water. A water wave is created when energy travels through water. Where does the energy come from? It usually comes from the wind hitting the water, but it could come from a child jumping in, or from a boat speeding by. In all cases energy is transferred to the water and moves through the water in waves.

When you stand on the shore to watch the waves, it looks like the water is traveling toward the shore. But it is the energy waves which are traveling, not the water. The water is simply moving up and down as the waves pass through it. The waves do not take the water with them. If they did, all the water would eventually be pushed onto the shore! The energy wave, not the water, rolls through the lake like a wheel toward the shore.

WHY DO WAVES BREAK?   We see only the top half of the energy wave. The other half of the energy wave is under the surface of the lake. When waves approach the shore, the bottom of the waves start to drag on the lake floor. This compresses the waves, making them taller and closer together. The waves finally get too tall and fall forward, or "break."

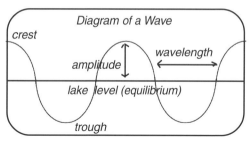

Diagram of a Wave

crest

amplitude

wavelength

lake level (equilibrium)

trough

1. What is a wave?

2. What is the most common cause of waves?

3. What rolls toward the shore in waves?

4. Why do waves break?

Use the diagram of a wave to help you match each term to its description.

5. amplitude   top of the wave

6. crest   bottom of the wave

7. trough   distance between crests

8. wavelength   distance from equilibrium
                       to the crest

PLEASE MAKE ME A LIST OF 10 ADJECTIVES THAT DESCRIBE WAVES. NOW MAKE A LIST OF 10 VERBS THAT ARE THINGS WAVES CAN DO.

The Ups and Downs of Lake Levels

The water is so low that the docks at Traverse Bay are too far above our boat to reach. The dockmaster had to lend us a rope ladder so we could get from the Blue Heron to the dock.

People often complain about changing lake levels. The water is too low to use an old boat dock. The water is too high and threatens to wash away a house. We need to remember that it is natural for lake levels to change. Climate controls lake levels. Changes in precipitation, evaporation, and runoff from the land make lake levels go up and down each season. Water is low in the winter when precipitation is in the form of snow. Levels rise in the spring when the snow melts and spring rains add water to the Great Lakes and to the streams which drain into the Great Lakes. During the summer, high temperatures make water evaporate from the lakes. Water levels also seem to rise and fall in a cycle of ten to twelve years. The wind can also change lake levels but only for a day or two. There is little people can do about naturally changing lake levels except to complain about them!

1. What natural event is the writer describing in this true account?

   "The water withdrew, leaving the ground dry, which had never before been visible, the fall of the water being equal to four perpendicular feet, and rushing back with great velocity above the common mark. It continued thus rising and falling for several hours, the commotion gradually decreasing until it remained stationary at its usual height."
   Unknown writer at Grand Portage, 1789

2. How are a surge and a seiche related?

3. What is the greatest factor in changing lake levels?

4. What happens to the lake levels during a year with little snow and a hot, dry summer? Why?

5. During what season is it most likely that a shoreline cottage will wash away? Why?

6. Circle all that are true. The water level in a Great Lake can change
   A) in a cycle of 10-12 years. B) season to season. C) day to day.

WIND / **LAKE WATER**

SURGE: *The wind blows continually in a certain direction over a long period of time, pushing the water to one end of a lake, often causing flooding.*

WATER / **WATER**

SEICHE: *A seiche (pronounced "saysh") occurs after a surge. When the wind stops, the water that was piled up on one end of the lake sloshes back and forth, from one end of the lake to the other, in large waves. This continues until the water returns to level.*

HERE'S A SONG ABOUT THE HYDROLOGIC CYCLE! SING IT TO THE TUNE OF "SHE'LL BE COMIN' ROUND THE MOUNTAIN."

WATER TRAVELS IN A CYCLE, YES IT DOES.
WATER TRAVELS IN A CYCLE, YES IT DOES.
IT GOES UP AS EVAPORATION, AND FORMS CLOUDS AS CONDENSATION,
THEN COMES DOWN AS PRECIPITATION, YES IT DOES!

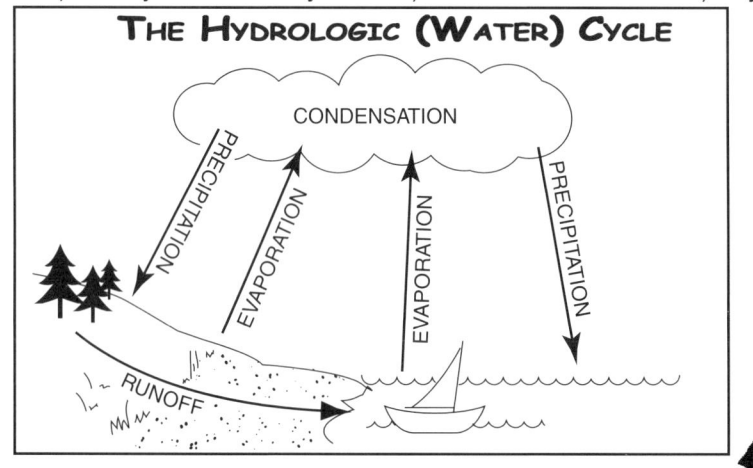

THE HYDROLOGIC (WATER) CYCLE

CONDENSATION

PRECIPITATION EVAPORATION EVAPORATION PRECIPITATION

RUNOFF

Shores Galore

Today we sailed on Lake Superior near Pictured Rocks and saw orange and red cliffs, caves, and even arches carved out of the sandstone by the wind and rain. It's a lot different from the other lakes we have been on. In Michigan I ran down the sand dunes and played on the beaches and another time I picked grapes at a vineyard that ran along the edge of Lake Erie. The shore there was made of dirt.

Different types of shores are found in different places depending on the geologic history of the area. The map below shows the main type of shores along each lake. Color in the map key using a different color for each type of shore. Then color the shorelines on the map to match the key.

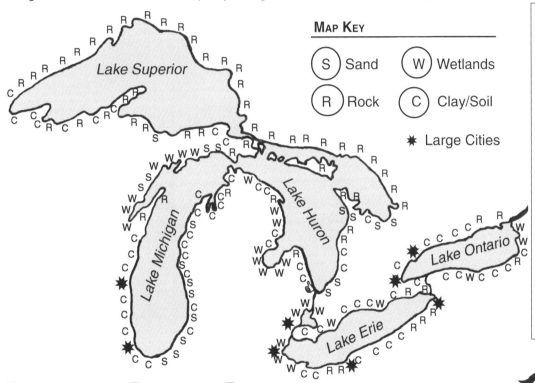

MAP KEY

(S) Sand   (W) Wetlands

(R) Rock   (C) Clay/Soil

✳ Large Cities

Use the letters in the map key to match each shore type to its description.

1. _____ The Canadian Shield, a huge slab of prehistoric bedrock, lies close to the surface of the earth here.

2. _____ The melting glaciers left behind bits of rock which were shaped into tiny grains by water and wind. Winds from the west piled the grains up on eastern shores to create dune areas.

3. _____ This shore is mainly fine sediment which settled out of retreating waters. It's a great place for people to build or grow things.

4. _____ Is it land or is it water? People aren't sure, but many birds and animals like to live here.

WHAT IS THE SHORELINE NEAREST WHERE YOU LIVE MADE OF? WRITE A PARAGRAPH DESCRIBING IT.

EXPERIMENT: EXPLORING EROSION

Take three pans and make an island in the center of each. Use a lump of damp soil from outdoors for one island, a rock for another, and a pile of sand for the third. Slowly pour a cup of water over each island. Watch what happens. Try pouring more water more quickly over each island.

1. Which erodes (washes away) fastest: sand, dirt, or rock?

2. Which will take longest to be eroded?

3. Look at the map again. Which lake is most likely to change shape in the next 500 years? Why?

4. Which lake is least likely to change? Why?

Moving Mountains of Sand

We stopped at Silver Lake, Michigan, and went on a dune buggy ride. The sand dunes here are huge, and they move! I saw treetops sticking out of them and some houses that were being buried in sand because the dune was flowing over them. Later we went to the beach on Lake Michigan and tried to catch antlions, but I never got one. I saw funny lines of black sand along the shore. I wonder what it is?

Bearberry

Scavenger Beetle

Antlion

Piping Plover

Beach Pea

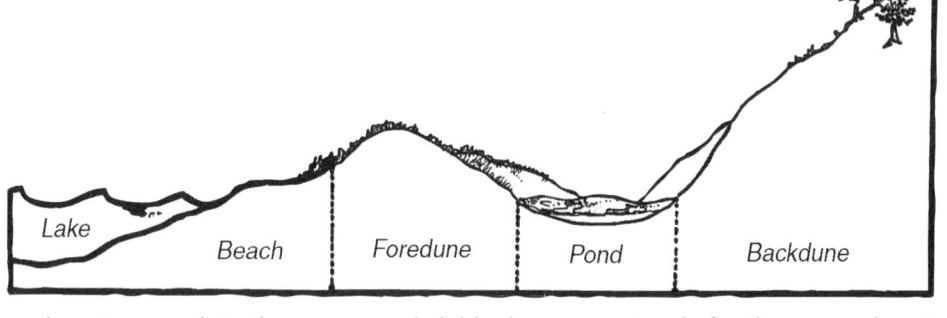

Lake | Beach | Foredune | Pond | Backdune

Answer the questions to complete the crossword. A black square stands for the space in a two-word answer. The illustrations will help you find the answers.

DOWN

1. This plant spreads over the sand to help stop sand from blowing. Part of its name is a veggie.
2. This bird is an endangered species. It builds a shallow nest on the beach.
4. Grr. This fierce insect digs a pit in the sand and waits at the bottom for its victims to fall in. It sucks the juices out of them and tosses the carcass out of the pit.
5. This plant has been around since prehistoric times. Its berries feed birds and mice.

ACROSS

1. This kind of dune often becomes wooded hills, inhabited first by pine trees, then by oak trees, and finally by beech and maple trees as the forest grows to cover it.
2. These low areas between dunes become homes for herons, toads, and other water animals.
3. This beetle searches the beach for dead fish, birds, and animals to eat.
6. A low ridge that runs close to shore and in front of larger dunes.

EXPERIMENT: MAGNETIC MAGNETITE

Have you ever seen a beach with bands of black sand running parallel to the water? The black particles are tiny grains of magnetite. It's an important iron ore. It is attracted to magnets, which is why it is named magnetite. See if you can pull it up out of the sand with a magnet.

MAP ACTIVITY

Find and label Sleeping Bear Dunes National Lakeshore (9G) and Indiana Dunes National Lakeshore (9K) on the Great Lakes Activity Map. To save space you may want to abbreviate National Lakeshore to N.L.

What Is a Wetland?

27 great blue herons. That's how many I counted today! We anchored near Point Pelee National Park, which is on the Canadian side of Lake Erie, and took the dinghy to get a closer look at the marsh. I brought my binoculars and saw lots of different birds, an otter, and some old muskrat houses. My dad said the park is on the migration routes of over 70 types of birds.

GREAT LAKES WETLANDS

A wetland is a land area covered with a shallow layer of water. There are many types of wetlands. Most wetlands in the Great Lakes area are freshwater marshes. They are open areas without many trees, but with many grasses, reeds, and other plants. The water level may change with the seasons or amount of rainfall. For many years people thought wetlands were worthless swamps. They were full of mosquitos, difficult to travel through or around, and no good for farming or building. People filled wetlands with dirt and built channels to drain the water out of them. You can probably think of places in your area where wetlands have been destroyed. Today two-thirds of the Great Lakes wetlands are gone.

Complete the statements. Use the information below each statement and the letters for help.

1. Wetlands are WATER P ___ R ___ ___ ___ ___ R ___.   (I F S I U E)
   Water trapped in wetlands is filtered of pollutants by the plants and soil. By the time water trickles down to our drinking water supply, it is clean.

2. Wetlands are FLOOD C ___ N ___ ___ ___LL ___ ___ S.   (T R O R O E)
   Wetlands can soak up a lot of extra water. This protects farmlands and cities from flooding during rainy seasons.

3. Wetlands are EROSION R ___ D U ___ ___ ___ ___.   (E E R C S)
   During storms, wetlands protect the land from waves that could wash the shore away.

4. Wetlands are WILDLIFE N U ___ ___ ___ R I E ___.   (E S R S)
   Many kinds of birds, fish, and animals raise their young in the safety of wetlands.

5. Wetlands are R ___ ___ T ___ ___ G PLACES.   (S N E I)
   Migratory birds depend on wetlands for places to stop and find abundant food, water, and shelter.

6. Wetlands are R ___ C R ___ ___ T ___ ___ N AREAS.   (O A I E E)
   Hunters, birdwatchers, fishermen, hikers, and photographers all enjoy the diverse and plentiful plants, fish, and animals that live in wetlands.

MAP ACTIVITY

Label these wetland areas on your Great Lakes Activity Map: Point Pelee National Park (N.P.) (13J), and Erie Marsh National Wildlife Area (N.W.A.) (12J).

ACTIVITY: MAKE YOUR OWN NATURE GUIDE BOOK

Learn about some plants and animals that live in wetlands. Make a guidebook by drawing or cutting out and pasting in a picture of each and writing down some facts about it. Here are some ideas: great blue heron, whistling swan, black duck, coot, Canada goose, otter, beaver, muskrat, cattail, duckweed, wild rice, green algae, leech, water spider, water strider, pitcher plant, yellow pond lily, water snake, peeper, leopard frog, painted turtle, snapping turtle, dragonfly, mosquito.

Rocky Places

We are sailing in Georgian Bay this summer, and it is totally different from Lake Michigan, where we were last summer. It has a wild, rocky shore with hundreds of little rock islands. The weather has worn some of the rock down into weird shapes. My mom says the rock here is limestone, which is easy for the wind and rain to wear down. I think that in places it looks like another planet.

PICTURED ROCKS NATIONAL LAKESHORE

Waterfalls plunge down tall sandstone cliffs into Lake Superior along Michigan's Upper Peninsula coastline. Minerals give the sandstone its lovely red, orange, and green colors while waves and wind shape it into arches and other formations.

GEORGIAN BAY ISLANDS NATIONAL PARK

Hundreds of rocky islands are in this huge bay, which is part of Lake Huron off Ontario's shore. Some islands are made of pink limestone that glaciers and waves carved into sharp points and unusual shapes.

NORTH CHANNEL

Sheltered by islands from the rough waters of Lake Huron, North Channel was canoed by explorers and traders. Today boaters thread their way through the wilderness channel, which is littered with uninhabited islands.

DOOR PENINSULA

This Wisconsin peninsula is a limestone ridge that juts out into Lake Michigan. Waves have carved caves, arches, and tall cliffs out of it. The French called the area "Death's Door" because its rocky waters were so dangerous to navigate.

Read about the places above and answer the questions.

1. Which place is made of sandstone?

2. Which places are made of limestone?

3. Which place has been used for centuries as a safe passageway for boats?

4. Which place was very dangerous for early water travelers?

5. What gives the Pictured Rocks their colors?

6. The Georgian Bay is part of Lake _____.

7. What natural forces have changed the stone of these rocky places into caves, cliffs and unusual shapes?

KNOW YOUR ROCKS!

If sandstone is made of sand, is limestone made of limes? No! Sandstone is made of sand which has hardened, but limestone is not made of limes! Limestone is made of the remains of billions of prehistoric sea plants and animals. These creatures were left behind by ancient saltwater seas which once covered the area.

MAP ACTIVITY

Find and label Pictured Rocks National Lakeshore (N.L.) (9D) and Georgian Bay Islands National Park (N.P.) (15E) on your Great Lakes Activity Map.

LEARN MORE ABOUT ONE OF THE PLACES ABOVE AND MAKE A TRAVEL POSTER OR BROCHURE ABOUT IT. INCLUDE PICTURES.

Islands of the Great Lakes

Today we stopped at Isle Royale National Park. Before it was a park, this island was used for copper mining and commercial fishing. Isle Royale was a hiding place, too. During the War of 1812, the British hid their ship Recovery in a bay on Isle Royale. The captain took down her masts, covered her with brush, and left her there undiscovered until the war ended.

MAP ACTIVITY   Isle Royale is one of many islands in the Great Lakes with interesting histories. Read about the Great Lakes islands below. Then use the coordinates to find and label these islands and Isle Royale (6B) on your Great Lakes Activity Map.

MACKINAC ISLAND

Back when most people around here traveled on the water, islands were good places for forts to defend the surrounding waterways. Fort Mackinac on Mackinac Island watched over Michigan's Straits of Mackinac. (11E)

MANITOULIN ISLAND

In the Great Lakes there are big islands and small. Manitoulin Island in Lake Huron is the largest freshwater island in the world. (13E)

JOHNSON'S ISLAND

An island is also a good place for a prison. During the Civil War, Confederate prisoners were kept on Johnson's Island in Lake Erie. (13K)

MANITOU ISLANDS

The Native Americans in the Great Lakes region had many stories about how islands were created. North and South Manitou islands in Lake Michigan, they said, are the spirits of two bear cubs who drowned crossing the lake, while Sleeping Bear Dunes is their mother, waiting for them on the shore. (9F)

BEAVER ISLAND

In the 1850s, James Jesse Strang picked Michigan's Beaver Island as the site for his Mormon settlement and named himself king of the island. (10E)

YOUR GREAT LAKES ISLAND

Look at a map of the Great Lake nearest where you live. Choose an island and answer the following questions about it.

1. What is the name of the island?

2. What is the nearest town on the mainland?

3. Does the map show ferry service to the island?

4. Describe the size and shape of the island.

5. Are there towns on it? What are they named?

6. How far is the island from shore?

7. Does the island have a natural harbor?

8. Find out more about your island. Check guidebooks, atlases, or the internet to see the island's population, its history, its special features, legends, parks, protected wildlife areas, forts, or monuments.

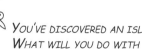

YOU'VE DISCOVERED AN ISLAND IN THE GREAT LAKES! WHAT WILL YOU NAME IT? WHAT WILL YOU DO WITH IT? DRAW ME A MAP OF IT.

Our Living Lakes

It's fun to just look at the shore as we sail on Lake Ontario. In some places there are dairy farms and vineyards along the shores. On the Canadian shore there are also big cities and factories. There is a lot of algae in the water. My mom said that's because the lake is polluted.

Before Europeans settled in the region the waters of the Great Lakes were clear and cool. Only a few nutrients from rotting plants entered the water. Streams running into the lakes were shaded by trees so their waters were cool. The lakes supported little life. All the lakes would be classified as *oligotrophic*. This word means "little food" or few nutrients.

Over the years human activities changed the lakes. Along the shores people cut trees, farmed, and built towns. Streams flowing into the lakes were no longer shaded by trees so their waters were warmer. They carried soil from land that had been cleared and sawdust from sawmills. Most importantly, fertilizers entered the lakes, putting extra nutrients in the water. The extra nutrients made more green plants and algae grow. Lake Erie changed so much that it became *mesotrophic*. Meso means "middle." The water contains some nutrients and supports some life.

More time passed. Factories and cities were built on the shores. Power plants dumped warm water into the lakes. Sewage and chemicals entered the water. Some of these pollutants added more nutrients. So many nutrients now polluted Lake Erie that it became *eutrophic*. This means "well-fed." The water has high levels of nutrients and supports much life.

It may seem like it would be good for a lake to be eutrophic and support much life, but it isn't. In this case it was a sign that man's activities were making the lake age too quickly. Eutrophic lakes have too much life—especially algae. The algae dies, sinks to the bottom, and rots. Decomposition uses up the oxygen in the water. Without enough oxygen, the fish die. Even though eutrophic means "much life," people began to call Lake Erie a dying lake. Pollution seemed to be bringing it to the end of its life cycle. Today people are working to clean up Lake Erie.

Now people are also concerned about Lake Ontario, which has changed from an oligotrophic lake to mesotrophic. When we look out over a Great Lake, we need to consider how our activities on the land are affecting the water and the creatures living in it. We need to protect all our lakes.

1. Before Europeans came to the area, all the lakes were what we would classify as _____ .

2. List four human activities which have changed the amount of life in the Great Lakes. Tell how each changed the water in the Lakes.

3. Explain why it is bad for a lake to be eutrophic.

4. What we do on the _____ affects the _____ .

5. *Triple Match:* Match each lake to two terms that describe it.

   oligotrophic   Lake Michigan   some life
                       Lake Erie
   mesotrophic   Lake Ontario   much life
                       Lake Huron
   eutrophic   Lake Superior   little life

   5 SYLLABLES
   7 SYLLABLES
   5 SYLLABLES

WRITE A HAIKU ABOUT SWIMMING IN OLIGOTROPHIC LAKE SUPERIOR. WRITE A HAIKU ABOUT SWIMMING IN EUTROPHIC LAKE ERIE. P.S. A HAIKU IS A JAPANESE POEM WITH 3 LINES. THE 1ST AND 3RD LINES HAVE 5 SYLLABLES. THE 2ND LINE HAS 7 SYLLABLES.

Something Fishy

Wow! I caught a four-pound lake trout in Lake Huron today! Mom cooked it for dinner. At first I didn't want to eat it, but it tasted good.

MEET A LAKE TROUT

Lake trout live in the Great Lakes. They are called "bony" fish because they have a skeleton made of bone like us. Trout are good to eat and are valuable for their meat. Most lake trout weigh three to nine pounds, but they can weigh up to 120 pounds. A lake trout can live up to 20 years. Use the underlined anatomy terms to label the lake trout.

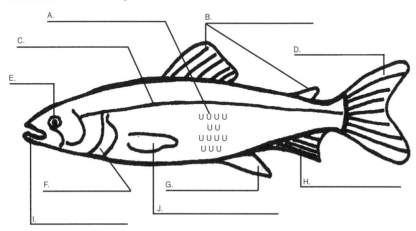

WHAT'S IT TO US?

We have more in common with a lake trout than you may think. Unscramble the words to find ways you are like a fish.

1. Nares are like my _____. (sislortn)

2. Gills are like my _____. (nulgs)

3. Scales are like my _____. (isnk)

4. Pectoral fins are like my _____. (sram)

5. We both have a bony _____. (ekselnot)

6. We can both _____ (aher), _____(ese), _____(lemsl), and _____. (elfe)

ANATOMY OF A BONY FISH

anal fin: On the underside of the fish near the tail.
caudal fin: The tail fin. It "steers" and moves the fish.
dorsal fins: On the top of the fish. Dorsal fins keep the fish's body from flopping sideways in the water.
pectoral fins: Fish have one on each side of their body just behind the head to propel themselves in the water, like we use arms.
ventral fins: A pair of fins on the underside of a fish.
eye: A fish sees in all directions because it has one eye on each side of its head.
mouth: May face up or down depending on the type of fish.
ears: Fish have ears, but they are hidden inside their bodies.
nares: Fish can smell with these sacs the way we can smell with our nostrils.
lateral line: A line of tiny holes which runs along each side of the fish from the gills to the tail. It helps a fish to feel movements in the water.
gills: Feathery flaps on the sides of the head. Oxygen enters the fish's blood through the gills.
opercle: A bony plate that covers the gills on a bony fish.
scales: They are made of bone and look like shingles on a roof. They are the "skin" of a fish.

IF YOU WERE A FISH, WHAT KIND WOULD YOU BE? WHAT WOULD YOU DO ALL DAY? MAKE UP A FISH ADVENTURE STORY.

Fabulous, Funny Fishes

I caught some minnows today. I scooped them up in my net and put them in a jar of water from the marsh. I like the way they dart around so quickly. I will let them go before I go to bed tonight.

You can tell a lot about how a fish lives just by looking at it. Use the information below to design your own fish. Pick out a body shape, mouth, tail, and other features. Draw your fish on a piece of paper and color it. Name it and write a paragraph describing it based on the features you gave it. What does it eat? How does it swim? Where does it hang out?

FISH FACTORY

BODY SHAPES

Torpedo
I swim fast and live in deep open water.

Flattened from side to side
I don't swim fast but can change direction quickly. I like to hide in cracks in rocks.

Eel-like
I glide easily through the water and can hide in very small places.

TAILS

Crescent-shaped
I swim fastest of all the fish and am always on the move.

Forked
I swim fast, but I don't swim all the time. (Hint: The deeper the fork of a fish's tail, the faster it can swim.)

Rounded
I usually take my time, but I might surprise you with a short burst of speed.

MOUTHS

Terminal
I like to chase things and catch them in my mouth.

Up-pointing
I like to eat things on the surface of the water.

Sub-terminal
I like to feed on the bottom.

Sucker mouth
I attach to other creatures and suck nutrients from them.

COLOR

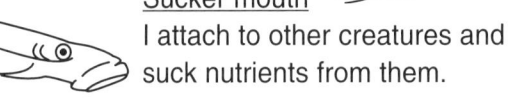

Countershading
I am a dark color on top and a light color on the bottom. Seen from above, I blend in with the dark water. Seen from below, my underside blends in with the sky above.

Disruptive Coloration
I have stripes, spots, or patterns on my body that visually break up my shape so I am harder to see.

Camouflage
I hide from predators by blending into my surroundings.

MORE FISH FEATURES

Barbels
My barbels are like feelers and are covered with taste buds. I use them to look for food on the bottom.

Big Eyes
I have big eyes because I am nocturnal and need to see in low light.

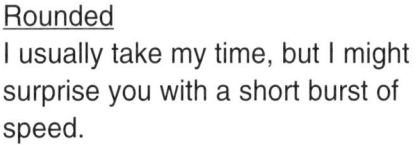

GO TO A PET STORE AND STUDY THE FISH. WHAT CAN YOU TELL ABOUT AN ANGEL FISH BY ITS SHAPE? A DANO BY ITS TAIL?

Lakeshore Birds of the Great Lakes

I finally saw a bald eagle. It was sitting high in a tree in the woods along a beach we visited. I was surprised to see an eagle near the beach, but when I looked it up in my bird book, I found out bald eagles like to eat dead fish that wash up on the shore.

Read the descriptions below and write the number by the bird it matches. Then color the picture based on the information in the description. You may want to use a bird book for help.

1. **Herring Gull** Adults have a white head and body with pale gray wings with black tips. Gulls like to rest on open water and ride the waves. They are scavengers.
2. **Spotted Sandpiper** This graceful long-legged bird runs along beaches bobbing its tail. In summer its underside is white with black spots. The rest of its body is olive-brown except for a white stripe above the eye.
3. **Bald Eagle** Look for a large brownish-black bird with a white tail and head, and yellow beak and feet. They are often perched high in a tree along the shore or soaring high in the sky looking for fish, rodents, or small birds to eat.
4. **Killdeer** Like sandpipers but plumper, killdeer have a white underside broken by two black bands across the neck. They have a brown head and back. They eat mosquitoes. Killdeer will pretend to have an injured wing to lure predators away from their nests.
5. **Common Loon** Often floating alone out on a lake, the loon has a lonely, haunting call and odd, quavering laugh. It has a distinctive black and white checkered back, black head with a broken band of white around the neck, and a long black beak.
6. **Black Tern** It looks like a gull except that it is dark in color and has a forked tail. Its head, beak, and underside are black, and its body is gray.

Marsh Birds of the Great Lakes

My grandma gave me a pair of binoculars before we set sail. I am getting better at identifying birds now that I can see them up close.

Read the descriptions below and write the number by the bird it matches. Then color the picture based on the information in the description. You may want to use a bird book for help.

1. **Belted Kingfisher** This smaller blue-gray bird with a white collar and breast has a large head and crest that make it easy to spot. It perches above the water waiting for a fish to pass by and then dives into the water to catch it.
2. **Great Blue Heron** This large blue-gray bird has a white crown and white on the front of its long neck. Blue herons are up to four feet tall and have stilt-like legs for wading in marshes, and a spear-like yellow bill for catching fish.
3. **American Bittern** Look for a small brown wading bird with black stripes running down its white breast. The top of its head and back of its neck are slate blue. When it senses danger it freezes with its bill pointing skyward.
4. **American Coot** It looks like a black duck with a white bill but does not have a webbed foot like a duck. Instead it has wavy flaps on each toe.
5. **Canada Goose** These large water birds with long black necks, white cheeks, and brown backs and wings run to take off from the water and fly in a V-formation.
6. **Mallard Duck** Female mallards are brown to camouflage them when nesting. The colorful males have a shiny green head and neck with a white ring around the neck, and purple-brown breast. The rest of the bird is brown except for two white bars on the wing and a blue tail.

IMAGINE YOUR ARE A BIRD SOARING HIGH ABOVE YOUR HOME AND COMMUNITY. WHAT WOULD YOU SEE? HOW WOULD YOU FEEL? WRITE ABOUT IT!

Special Effects: Great Lakes Weather and Climate

Sailing wasn't very good today because there wasn't much wind, so we went swimming off the boat. Later in the afternoon we caught a lake breeze and the sailing was great!

If you have spent any time in the Great Lakes region, you have heard people use certain terms and expressions to describe the climate and the weather, like *lake effect snow*, *lake breeze*, *fruit belt*, and *high humidity*. They are talking about the effect the big lakes have on our weather and climate, especially along the eastern shores of the lakes. Winds from the west move air masses and weather across the lakes, impacting the climate on the eastern shores. Read about the factors that cause our weather and climate and draw a line from the cause to its effects. Each cause has three effects.

CAUSE OF THE WEATHER OR CLIMATE

A. The Great Lakes are huge bodies of water. They cool down and warm up very slowly as the seasons change. They are cooler than the air during the summer and warmer than the air during the winter months.

B. When air masses move over a Great Lake they pick up moisture from the lake. The moisture is often released as rain or snow.

LAKE EFFECT PRECIPITATION

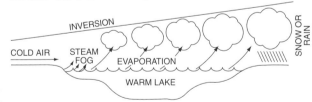

EFFECT ON THE WEATHER OR CLIMATE

1. The Great Lakes region is cooler in the summer and warmer in the winter than other areas at the same latitude.

2. During the summer the humidity or moisture in the air is usually high.

3. The Great Lakes states receive more snow and rain than other areas at the same latitude. In Michigan it either rains or snows one out of every three days.

4. On hot summer days the air over the land becomes very warm and begins to rise. Cooler air from over the lake flows inland to take its place and creates a "lake breeze" toward the shore.

5. Winters tend to have many cloudy days.

6. Belts of land along the lakeshores are perfect for growing fruit like grapes, peaches, and cherries. Cool spring weather keeps the fruit trees and vines from blooming until all danger of frost is past. Warm falls give the fruit time to ripen.

MAP ACTIVITY Use your Great Lakes Activity Map to locate five cities which experience lake effect weather. List these cities below.

 HAVE YOU VISITED ANY OF THE GREAT LAKES? WHICH ONES? TELL ME ABOUT YOUR VISIT AND DRAW ME A PICTURE OF SOMETHING YOU SAW THERE.

Island in the Crossroads: Mackinac Has Seen It All

Today we visited Mackinac Island, Michigan. It's a state park where no cars are allowed, so everyone travels by bike, horse, or foot! We ate the island's famous fudge, went in historic buildings, then toured Fort Mackinac. This island was crowded with tourists, and from what I learned at the fort, it has been a pretty busy place all through history! The Straits of Mackinac has been called the great crossroads of the north. It is where all the Great Lakes trade routes of the Native Americans met. From the 1600s through the 1800s, there were French and English fur traders and soldiers, priests and explorers here. Then the tourists started coming, and they haven't stopped. Just think what this island has seen! I wish it could talk.

"I have never been lonely. Throughout history, people have lived in my forests, visited my harbors, and glided past my shores through the sparkling Straits of Mackinac. For many, many years I was the home of the **Ottawa** people. They lived on me and on the lands beyond my shores. They visited me to trade and fish. Back then, only birchbark canoes floated past me.

"In 1634, French explorer **Jean Nicolet** passed by on his way from Georgian Bay to Lake Michigan. He was searching for a route to China, but he ended up in Green Bay! Missionaries began to come, too. They wanted to teach the Native Americans about their god. The French missionary **Père Marquette** came here in 1671 before building his mission across the water at St. Ignace. Two years later I saw him leave St. Ignace with French explorer **Louis Jolliet** in bark canoes to explore the Mississippi River.

"A few years later, in 1679, I saw the first sailing ship pass through the Straits. The *Griffin* was built by the French explorer **LaSalle** and was sailing to Green Bay to pick up a load of furs to take back to Montreal. It was the first boat other than a canoe ever to touch the upper Great Lakes. On its return trip, it vanished without a trace, the first of many **Great Lakes shipwrecks**.

"In 1781, British soldiers built a fort on me! They destroyed their old Fort Michilimackinac that sat on the northern tip of lower Michigan and built a new Fort Mackinac right here on my bluff overlooking the Straits, where they thought it could be better defended. What did they need to defend? The **fur trade**. Trapping animals for their furs was big business around here in the 1700s and 1800s. I saw many **voyageurs** pass by over those years, their big canoes full of bales of furs. In fact, John Jacob Astor built his American Fur Company headquarters right here in 1809.

"In 1819, ***Walk-in-the-Water***, the first steam-ship on the Great Lakes, passed by. Then came the **immigrants**, looking for new homes in towns all along the Great Lakes shores. They came by boat from the East, through the **Erie Canal** and on up through the lakes. From 1840 to 1860 Southern slaves made their way to freedom along **Underground Railroad** routes that passed my shores. In the 1840s **copper miners** passed me on their way to the western Upper Peninsula to mine the copper there.

"In the 1850s, people began building summer cottages on me. I guess they noticed my lovely summer climate and beautiful views. After the Civil War, hotels and more homes were built. By 1895, most of me was a state park, and my fort belonged to the state as well. From then on, more and more **tourists** came by ferry boat, and businesses prospered.

"In the 1950s I watched as a five-mile-long bridge was built across the Straits connecting the two peninsulas of Michigan. The **Mackinac Bridge** was the longest suspension bridge in the world then, and now it carries some five million vehicles every year. The Straits is a busy water highway full of pleasure boats and huge **freighters**. About 900,000 tourists visit me each year.

"Nope, I have never been lonely."

PICK A PROJECT

Choose one of the projects below to help you learn more about the Great Lakes.

MAKE A REPORT

Pick one of the bold words or phrases from the text and learn all you can about it using this book and any other sources you can find. Then write a report telling everything you learned. You may draw pictures or maps to go with it if you like.

MAKE A GREAT LAKES PRIMER

A primer (rhymes with *shimmer*) is a book of basic facts for young children. Find out the most important fact about each bold phrase. Why was that person or thing important in Great Lakes history? Write a sentence or two about each bold item. Illustrate your primer if you like.

MAKE A TIMELINE

Use the information in the text to create a timeline of the people and things which passed by the island.

WHAT GROUPS OF PEOPLE LIVED WHERE YOU NOW LIVE 100, 200, OR 300 YEARS AGO? FIND OUT!

Goals of the Great Lakes Explorers

I always thought it would be cool to be the first person to explore a place—like the French explorers who were the first Europeans to come to the Great Lakes. Then my dad goes and spoils the whole idea. Exploring was very dangerous, he says, and the explorers were not out there for the fun of it. They had other goals.

- *Some wanted to change the Indians' religion to Christianity.*
- *Some were looking for a water route across North America to the Pacific Ocean and on to China.*
- *Some wanted to claim land in North America for France.*
- *Some wanted to build the fur trade for France by establishing trading posts. In the process, they also hoped to become rich.*

Read about the following explorers. Then put their names (underlined) in the box or boxes on the next page that best describe their goals.

Samuel de Champlain

The French king sent Champlain to North America to build the fur trade. He established a settlement called Quebec in 1608. From there he explored Lake Ontario and went as far west as Lake Huron in search of the Northwest Passage.

Jean Nicolet

This explorer was the first Frenchman to explore Lake Michigan. In 1634 he thought he had reached China, but what he actually found was the land we now call Wisconsin!

Etienne Brulé

This young man was sent by Champlain in 1622 to find a water route across the continent. He explored Lake Huron and probably went into Lake Superior as well.

Père Marquette

This Jesuit priest set up two missions in what is now Michigan's Upper Peninsula. In 1673 he also explored the Mississippi River with Louis Jolliet, hoping that the great river would lead to the Pacific Ocean.

Robert Cavelier, Sieur de LaSalle

This Frenchman ran a fur trading post at Fort Frontenac. He then built a sailing vessel called the *Griffin* and sailed from eastern Lake Erie to Lake Michigan's Green Bay. There LaSalle loaded the ship with furs and sent it back to Fort Frontenac. The ship was lost and never found again. LaSalle went on to the Mississippi where he claimed the territory for France. He hoped to build a huge fur trading empire for his country.

Louis Hennepin

Although he is best remembered for his writings (published in 1697) about Niagara Falls and the adventures of LaSalle, Hennepin was a priest who accompanied LaSalle and other explorers.

Daniel Greysolon, Sieur Duluth

An explorer who wanted to find a passage to the Pacific, Duluth ended up founding a fur trading post in 1686. He also served as peacemaker for the Indians who sometimes made fur trading difficult.

Claude Allouez

This Jesuit priest had missions along Lake Michigan and Lake Superior in the 1660s. He also tried to collect information about the Mississippi River and its outlet.

Pierre Esprit Radisson & Médart Chouart, Sieur de Groseilliers

These fur traders explored the shores of Lake Superior beginning in 1658 and returned two years later with loads of furs and knowledge of geography and fur resources in the region.

Adrien Jolliet

Until this explorer learned from the Indians in 1669 that he could travel from Lake Superior to Lake Huron to Lake Erie and portage to Lake Ontario, the French did not know the Great Lakes created a natural water route. Jolliet had been sent by the French government to search for copper along the shores of Lake Superior.

CLAIMING LAND & RESOURCES FOR FRANCE	BUILDING THE FUR TRADE	LOOKING FOR A WATER ROUTE TO THE PACIFIC	BRINGING CHRISTIANITY TO THE INDIANS

Who were the early explorers or settlers in your area? Find out!

A Fortune in Furs

We made it to Thunder Bay, Ontario, just in time for the Great Rendezvous! At Old Fort William the year is always 1816, and every July they reenact the annual rendezvous of the fur trade days.

The North American fur trade, begun in the 17th century by the French, was at its peak during the 18th and 19th centuries. Europeans wanted fur, especially beaver, to make hats and other clothing. Native Americans wanted trade goods like iron tools, guns, and wool blankets. Around 1800, the North West Company in Montreal controlled 80% of the fur trade. The company was owned by a group of partners (called *bourgeois*) who became very wealthy running various parts of the business. They employed many people at that time, including 50 clerks, 70 interpreters, 35 guides, and 1,102 canoemen called voyageurs. The voyageurs were hired to paddle large canoes thousands of miles along a network of rivers, lakes, and streams throughout the wild interior of the Great Lakes region. They took trade goods to the Native Americans to exchange for furs, then returned with the tons of pelts. The voyageurs were the transportation muscle of the fur trade.

The fur trade followed an annual cycle and the high point of the year was rendezvous time. Each July the North West Company held its rendezvous at a fort in Grand Portage along the northwest coast of Lake Superior. Northern voyageurs, or *hivernants* (winterers), brought the previous winter's furs from trading posts throughout the interior to be counted, sorted, and weighed. Montreal voyageurs brought trade goods for the next winter's trading. After the rendezvous, the hivernants returned to their posts with the trade goods, and the Montreal voyageurs returned to Montreal with the furs. North West Company officials, partners, and clerks all met at the Grand Portage rendezvous, too, for an annual business meeting and to oversee the exchange of furs and goods. The voyageur's life was a hard and dangerous one. The annual rendezvous was also an occassion for eating, drinking and socializing.

THE VOYAGEURS

Most of the voyageurs were French-Canadian, but some were metis (mixed Native American and European) and some were Native American. To fit into a canoe and paddle all day, voyageurs needed to be short and strong. They were a proud and colorful group, dressing in brightly colored hats and sashes. A good singing voice was a prized characteristic, as the voyageurs often sang as they paddled. While the partners of the North West Company were making fortunes, the voyageurs worked for very low wages.

THE JOB

Voyageurs paddled 16-18 hours a day, approximately 40-60 paddle strokes per minute. Depending on conditions, breaks were taken every 45 minutes to two hours. These resting times were called pipes, because the men generally smoked their clay pipes while relaxing for 10-15 minutes. These irregular breaks were used to measure distances; a particular lake might be a six-pipe crossing, for example. Canoes traveled in brigades of usually four to eight. Each canoe had a bowsman at the front, a steersman with a long paddle standing at the rear, and several pairs of middlemen sitting in the middle of the canoe doing most of the paddling. The voyageurs' routes included many portages. Rapids or other obstacles in the water meant that the canoes had to be taken ashore, emptied, and carried, along with their cargo and supplies, along trails past the obstacle. Furs were in 90-pound bales; a voyageur carried two at a time, usually at a brisk trot. Speed was important. The journey to Grand Portage from either direction took about two months, so a round trip risked running into fall freeze-ups. During their summer-long journey, the voyageurs ate two meals a day, usually corn mush and pork fat for the Montreal voyageurs and pemmican (dried, powdered buffalo meat mixed with lard) for the hivernants. In the evening the voyageurs came ashore, emptied their canoes and inspected them for damage, and made any necessary repairs. They used their canoes for shelter at night, turning them on their sides and propping them up with paddles.

THE CANOES

To men making a fortune in the fur trade, speedy and reliable transportation of goods was essential. Canoes were ideal on the lakes and surrounding rivers because of their speed and light weight for portaging. Voyageur canoes were large versions of traditional Native American birch bark canoes. The hivernants of the North West Company used the North canoe, which was 18 to 22 feet long and could carry up to 6 voyageurs and some 3,000 pounds of furs, food, and supplies. Empty, it could be carried by 2 men. The Montreal voyageurs used the larger Montreal canoe, which was 30 to 40 feet long and about 6 feet wide in the middle. It could carry up to 8,000 pounds of trade goods and provisions and 8 to 16 voyageurs. The Montreal could weigh upwards of 200 pounds empty and required several men to portage. Canoes were much lighter in weight than other types of boats and were maneuverable in most conditions. Although easily damaged, they could be repaired along the way. The lifespan of a voyageur canoe was one to two years.

FIGURE IT OUT:

1. In 1803, the North West Company made 197,695 pounds sterling (the currency of the United Kingdom at the time). At that time, one pound equaled about five US dollars. How much money did they make in US dollars?

2. If the US dollar is worth about 14 times more today than it was in 1803, how much money did they make in today's US dollars?

3. It took voyageurs about two months to make the 450-mile journey from Montreal to Grand Portage described in the Map Activity. About how many miles did they average per day?

MAP ACTIVITY

Mark the route of the Montreal voyageurs on your Great Lakes Activity Map. First find Montreal. Draw a red line from Montreal along the Ottawa River and through Lake Nipissing. Continue the line through the North Channel of Lake Huron, through the St. Marys River into Lake Superior, then along the north coast of Lake Superior to Grand Portage. Add the red line to your map's legend, labeling it "North West Company canoe route, Montreal to Grand Portage." Imagine paddling this huge distance in a canoe!

ACTIVITY: BE A VOYAGEUR!

In a big area, like a playground or gym, make the outline of a North or Montreal canoe according to the measurements given. You could use tape on the floor or chalk on cement. Put the appropriate number of kids in to be the voyageurs. They should kneel in pairs and hold rulers as paddles. Have a teacher or parent call out "stroke" 40 to 60 times per minute and time them as they paddle. How long can they keep it up? Remember, smooth paddling is important. You're carrying someone else's fortune, and carelessness on the water can be deadly!

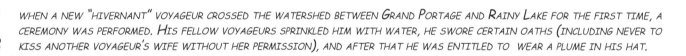

WHEN A NEW "HIVERNANT" VOYAGEUR CROSSED THE WATERSHED BETWEEN GRAND PORTAGE AND RAINY LAKE FOR THE FIRST TIME, A CEREMONY WAS PERFORMED. HIS FELLOW VOYAGEURS SPRINKLED HIM WITH WATER, HE SWORE CERTAIN OATHS (INCLUDING NEVER TO KISS ANOTHER VOYAGEUR'S WIFE WITHOUT HER PERMISSION), AND AFTER THAT HE WAS ENTITLED TO WEAR A PLUME IN HIS HAT.

By the Shores of Gitche Gumee: Native People of the Great Lakes

> "By the shores of Gitche Gumee,
> By the shining Big-Sea-Water,
> Stood the wigwam of Nokomis,
> Daughter of the Moon, Nokomis."

My mom likes to recite lines from the famous poem The Song of Hiawatha which was written by Henry Wadsworth Longfellow in 1855 and set along the shores of Lake Superior (Gitche Gumee). Sometimes I squint my eyes and imagine I see a village of wigwams along the shore. I'm trying to learn who the native people were who lived around these Great Lakes.

Read about the Native American tribes that lived in the Great Lakes area when Europeans first arrived. Select the number on the map that best shows the tribes' locations and write it in the space provided.

_____ **Ojibwa** (Ojibwe or Chippewa) were especially good at building birch bark canoes. They lived both north and south of Lake Superior.

_____ **Iroquois** were a very powerful group or nation made up of five tribes along the southern shore of Lake Ontario. The Iroquois stopped French explorers and traders from moving freely on the eastern Great Lakes for many years.

_____ **Huron** (Wendat or Wyandotte) were made up of four tribes and were dispersed throughout the region by their enemies, the Iroquois.

_____ **Neutrals** lived south of Lake Ontario and north of Lake Erie. They did not want to be involved in the wars between the Huron and Iroquois, so the French named them "Neutrals."

_____ **Erie** lived on the southwestern end of Lake Erie. The tribe was destroyed by the Iroquois in the 1650s.

_____ **Menominee** lived on the northwest side of Lake Michigan. They gathered wild rice along the northern lakeshore.

_____ **Miami** lived along southern Lake Michigan and the Detroit River before moving farther south to what is now Indiana.

_____ **Odawa** (Ottawa) were traders who lived at the straits connecting Lake Michigan and Lake Huron. In the 1700s they also lived near what is now Detroit.

_____ **Potawatomi** lived on both sides of Lake Michigan.

READ AN INDIAN LEGEND OR A STORY ABOUT GREAT LAKES INDIANS AND REWRITE IT AS A PLAY. ACT IT OUT WITH YOUR FRIENDS!

By the Boatload: Immigrants Come to the Great Lakes

The Great Lakes have been like a water highway for travelers all through history. Immigrants from many countries traveled by boat to their new homes around the Great Lakes.

READ THESE ACCOUNTS OF IMMIGRANTS TRAVELING THE GREAT LAKES BY STEAMBOAT IN THE 19TH CENTURY:

A A group of emigrants collected around a stove, where an English mother nursing her infant, a child lying asleep upon a mastiff, and a long-bearded German smoking his meerschaum...were the only complete figures amid an indefinite number of heads, arms, and legs lying about in the whimsical confusion.
(Charles Fenno Hoffman, *A Winter in the West, I* , 1834)

B That short man yonder, with square shoulders and a crooked pipe in his mouth...that man had probably not the slightest idea of the kind of country he was coming to. His eyes are now just opening to his new condition.... That man has not yet a thought in common with the people of his new abode around him. He looks, indeed, as if he came from another planet. Visit him on his thriving farm ten years hence, and, except in the single point of language, you will find him (unless he has settled among a nest of his countrymen) at home with his neighbors, and happily conforming to their usages. (Hoffman)

C Here, on the pier, I see disembarking the Germans, the Norwegians, the Swedes, the Swiss. Who knows how much of old legendary lore, of modern wonder, they have already planted amid the Wisconsin forests? Soon, soon their tales of the origin of things...will be so mingled with those of the Indian, that the very oak trees will not know them apart.
(Margaret Fuller, *Summer on the Lakes, in 1843*)

D Here lie stretched in wild disorder & confusion upon the floor like the slain on the field of battle in all shapes & positions...the man of gray hairs & the tender infant, the rosy cheeked damsel & the sturdy wood chopper. Here is crying & scolding & snoring & groaning. Some in berths & some on chairs & trunks & settees & the rest on the floor. Some sitting & some lying, some dressed & some undressed, some covered & some uncovered and naked; some are stretched on beds, others on matrasses & cushions & cloaks & not a few are trying to find the soft side of the hard floor. Such is a steamboat life on Lake Erie, a scene which I do not soon wish to experience again. (Charles Minton Baker, *Journal from Vermont to Wisconsin, 1838*)

NOW ANSWER THE FOLLOWING QUESTIONS ON A SEPARATE PIECE OF PAPER.

1. Look up these words in a dictionary and write down their definitions: **immigrant**, **emigrant**, **mastiff**, **meerschaum**, **abode**, **hence** ("ten years hence"), **disembarking**, **mingled**, **slain**, and **berths**.

2. Passages A and D talk about "heads, arms, and legs lying about" and "the slain on the field of battle." What are they actually describing? Do the words they use help you to imagine the scene? Describe in your own words what these steamboat trips might have been like.

3. The last sentence of B and the last sentence of C both predict the same future for immigrants coming to the United States. Explain what that is.

WHERE DID YOUR FAMILY'S ANCESTORS COME FROM? HOW DID THEY GET HERE? WHY DID THEY CHOOSE TO SETTLE WHERE THEY DID?

Songs & Stories of the Great Lakes

We bought a CD of Great Lakes folksongs and listened to it tonight. It had songs about lighthouses, shipwrecks, mining, and lumbering on it. Some of the songs are very funny, but my mom said some of them are "inappropriate for young ears." I thought those were the funniest!

For centuries the lakes have been shaping the lives of people who live on their shores and work on their waters. The influence of the lakes is shown in the many legends, stories, poems, and songs people have created about the Great Lakes. Read the excerpts below to experience some legends, songs, and stories of the Great Lakes.

An Indian Legend: "The Storms on Lake Michigan"
When Native Americans saw storms on the lakes, they created this legend to explain the source of the storms.

> *Long, long ago a wicked manitou [spirit] dwelt in the country above Little Traverse Bay. He was called Motche Manitou. One day the people held a council, and decided to put a stop to his evil deeds. They took Motche Manitou and threw him into the bay. There he lies to this day. Once in a while he tries to get out. Then the water is disturbed, and furious storms rage over the lake.*

Johanna R.M. Lyback, Indian Legends, Lyons and Carnahan, Chicago, 1925, p. 164-165.

A Tall Tale: "Paul Bunyan Harnesses Lake Superior"
Tall tales were inspired by the enormous waters and wild forests of the region—it seemed that anything could happen in the Great Lakes.

> *[Paul Bunyan] decided to carry his timber products to market in his own freighter, and he built and launched the largest ship that ever sailed on Lake Superior. Its capacity was equal to that of ten ordinary lumber carriers . . . The masts of the Paul Bunyan were so tall that the officers had to use telescopes when looking aloft at the sailors in the crow's nest, and they didn't shout orders to the sailors up there, they telephoned them. The topmasts were hinged and they could be lowered to let the clouds go by . . . .*

Stanley D. Newton, Paul Bunyan of the Great Lakes, Avery Color Studios, AuTrain, Michigan, 1985, p. 76.

A Great Lakes Folksong: "The Julie Plante"
Mariners celebrated their hard lives and mourned those lost on the lakes with shipping folksongs. This song is written in French-Canadian English.

1. On wan dark night on de Lake St. Clair De win' she blow, blow, blow,
   An' de crew of de wood-scow *Julie Plante* Got scar' an run below.
   For de win' she blow like Hurricane, By'n by she blow some more,
   Ad de scow bus' up jus' off Grosse Point ten acres from de shore.

5. Now, all good wood scow sailormen, Take warnin' by dat storm,
   An' go marree some nice French girl, An leeve on wan beeg farm.
   De win' may blow like hurriane An' s'pose she blow some more,
   You can't get drown on Lake St. Clair So long you stay on shore.
   by W.H. Drummond

A Voyageur Paddling Song: "Entendez-Vouz?"
(or, "Do You Hear?")
Voyageurs used chants and songs to keep a steady paddling rhythm for the long journeys on the lakes.

> *Entendezvous sur l'ormeau, Chanter le petite oi-seau,*
> *Do you hear the little bird, Singing on the sapling elm?*
>
> *Tra-la- la-la- la-la- la-la- la, La-la- la La-la-la.*

WRITE a legend, song or poem, or tall tale about the Great Lakes. Use the guidelines below, be creative, and have fun!
  A legend usually explains something in nature and often has animals, birds or fish as characters. They might have a problem to solve and could be hindered or helped by a spirit.
  A song or poem might describe an experience you have had or even something you have seen. Include lots of adjectives to make it interesting and describe your feelings, too—free, sad, calm, etc.
  A tall tale is a silly story which uses hyperbole, or lots of obvious exaggeration. You can make the impossible happen and it's OK!

Mackinac the Beautiful: A Listening Activity

My dad is reading me an old book called A Summer in the Wilderness *by Charles Lanman. He was a travel writer in the 1840s. He uses a lot of words we don't use now, but it's cool because he talks about what a great tourist spot Mackinac Island is. I had to remind myself that what he wrote is more than 150 years old!*

Listen to the reading on the CD-ROM. Use a blank piece of paper to take notes. Then come back to this page and answer the questions.

1. Three lakes that wash the shores of Mackinac Island are
   A. Erie, Huron, and Michigan.
   B. Ontario, Superior, and Huron.
   C. Superior, Michigan, and Huron.
   D. Huron, Erie, and Ontario.

2. The author says that steamers from these cities stopped at the island:
   A. Detroit and Milwaukee.
   B. Milwaukee and Chicago.
   C. Duluth and Chicago.
   D. Detroit and Chicago.

3. On the top of the bluff overlooking the island was a
   A. Indian camp.
   B. fort.
   C. city.
   D. hotel.

4. The writer believes that the tourists who come to the island will do all of the following except
   A. spoil its original glory.
   B. want to come back.
   C. visit in winter.
   D. enjoy it.

5. In this letter the word *larders* means
   A. storerooms.
   B. fats.
   C. big people.
   D. fish.

6. The natives on the beach were NOT
   A. attacking the fort.
   B. repairing their canoes.
   C. cooking.
   D. playing games.

7. To this writer the island appears to be a natural
   A. park.
   B. place for a city.
   C. fortress.
   D. winter resort.

8. One way that Mackinac Island in 1846 was different from Mackinac Island today is
   A. its beautiful, clear water.
   B. its scenery.
   C. its fort.
   D. its Indian encampment.

9. The writer describes the island's geography as
   A. having a high bluff.
   B. a rocky beach.
   C. basically flat.
   D. having only a small cove for docking.

10. The writer says the following things can be found on the island:
    A. turtles.
    B. bears.
    C. trading houses.
    D. palm trees.

IMAGINE LIVING ON MACKINAC ISLAND. MAKE A LIST OF TEN ADJECTIVES THAT DESCRIBE MACKINAC ISLAND DURING THE SUMMER MONTHS. MAKE A LIST OF TEN ADJECTIVES THAT DESCRIBE MACKINAC ISLAND DURING THE WINTER MONTHS.

From Dugouts to Diesel

When I watch the other boats go by, it seems like I can see every kind of boat there is on the Great Lakes. But Mom and Dad say that many more kinds of boats have come and gone throughout history. They say that people who live near water have always built boats. The kinds they build depend on what materials they have to work with and what they want to use the boats for. Here are some of the different kinds of boats people have built and used in the Great Lakes region.

> **"IRON IN THE WATER SHALL FLOAT**
> **AS EASY AS A WOODEN BOAT."**
> *(Prediction of Mother Shipton, 17th-century prophetess.)*

PADDLE POWER!
Dugout canoes were built for transportation by the Old Copper Indians in the Lake Superior area some 5,000 years ago. A log was dug out with copper tools or burned out. **Bark canoes** of the Great Lakes Indians were usually made of a birch bark skin stretched over cedar ribs, then sewn with fir roots and sealed with resin. Larger versions were used in the fur trade.

WIND POWER!
The first sailing ships that appeared on the Great Lakes in 1679 were **square-rigged sailing ships.** Their sails were arranged crosswise. By the mid-1800s, **schooners** were the preferred cargo carrier on the Great Lakes because they could be operated by a smaller crew. Schooners' sails ran in line with the boat, like today's sailboats. They ranged in size from under 100 feet to over 200 feet.

NUMBER THESE VESSELS TO SHOW THEIR CHRONOLOGICAL ORDER AND LABEL THEM USING THE VESSEL NAMES IN BOLD. THE FIRST ONE IS DONE FOR YOU.

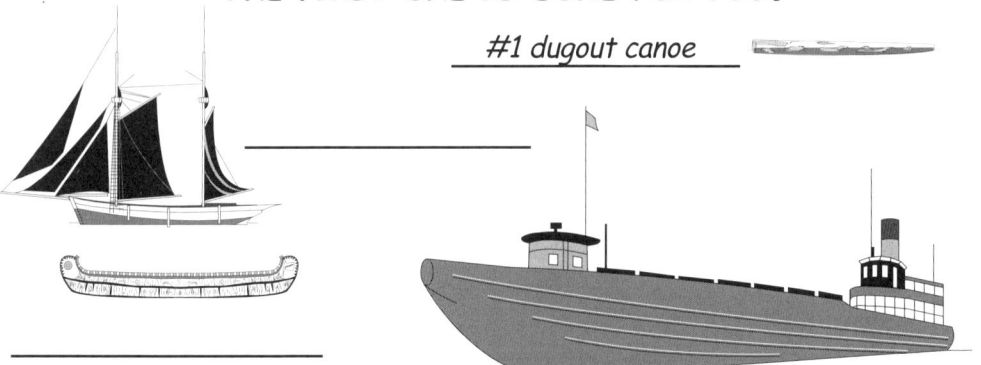

#1 dugout canoe

STEAM POWER!
In 1816 the first **steamships** appeared on the lakes. Steam engines that burned wood (and later coal) powered big paddle wheels on either side of the boat. These early steamers were made of wood and carried cargo and passengers. In the 1880s Great Lakes steamships began to be built with iron hulls. During the 1890s, the **whaleback** was a popular design for cargo carriers. Some were over 400 feet long. With their rows of cargo hatches on top, they looked more like modern freighters than anything so far.

FUEL POWER!
Freighters on the Great Lakes today are between 500 and 1,000 feet long. They are diesel or turbine powered and carry bulk or general cargo.

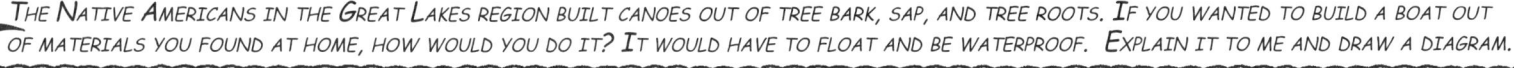

THE NATIVE AMERICANS IN THE GREAT LAKES REGION BUILT CANOES OUT OF TREE BARK, SAP, AND TREE ROOTS. IF YOU WANTED TO BUILD A BOAT OUT OF MATERIALS YOU FOUND AT HOME, HOW WOULD YOU DO IT? IT WOULD HAVE TO FLOAT AND BE WATERPROOF. EXPLAIN IT TO ME AND DRAW A DIAGRAM.

The Fish Biz: Commercial Fishing on the Great Lakes

We're in Lake Erie and today I saw a fishing boat pulling in its trap nets full of fish. Mom said they're probably walleye—yum! In commercial fishing, Lake Erie is the most productive of all the Great Lakes.

Residents of the Great Lakes region have always fished the lakes for food. Commercial fishing, catching fish to sell, started on the Great Lakes around 1820. The largest fish harvests recorded on the lakes were way back in 1889 and 1899, but even then some species were declining in numbers. Today the Great Lakes fishery (that means a fishing area or the fishing industry) includes some native species and some that have been introduced, either accidentally or on purpose. The lakes are regularly restocked with certain species that are raised in fish hatcheries. Fish commonly caught include lake trout, salmon, walleye, yellow perch, whitefish, small-mouth bass, steelhead, and brown trout. The alewife is harvested for animal feed.

Most commercial fishing operations use nets to catch fish. One type is a gill net, which hangs like a fence in the water. When a fish is too big to swim through the net's mesh, it is caught by its gills and dies. Most nets used today are trap nets. These nets form tunnels that lead fish to a central enclosure. When the trap nets are raised, the live fish are sorted and recreational species thrown back.

Today the Great Lakes fishery is threatened by pollution, overfishing, and invader species. Some native species are extinct. To solve these problems, fishing is carefully regulated.

ANSWER THE QUESTIONS AND THEN USE THE NUMBERS TO FIND THE NAME OF A FISH THAT IS A POPULAR COMMERCIAL CATCH IN ALL OF THE GREAT LAKES.

___ ___ ___ ___ ___ ___ ___ means a place where fish are caught or the fishing industry.
 1   2   3   4   5   6   7

___ ___ ___ ___ ___ ___ ___ ___ ___ is one of the three threats to commercial fishing in the Great Lakes.
 8   9   10   10   11   12   2   9   13

The ___ ___ ___ ___ ___ ___ ___ is caught for use as animal feed.
    14   10   5   15   2   1   5

Some species of fish are raised in a fish ___ ___ ___ ___ ___ ___ ___ to stock the lakes.
                                         4   14   12   16   4   5   6   7

ANSWER: ___ ___ ___ ___ ___ ___ ___ ___ ___ ___ ___
         7   5   10   10   9   15   8   5   6   16   4

IN THE GREAT LAKE NEAREST YOU, WHICH KINDS OF FISH ARE CAUGHT COMMERCIALLY? FIND OUT!

Charting Our Course

Sailing our boat around the Great Lakes is a lot like driving a car from place to place. We have special maps that show us the way. There are buoys and markers in the water that act like traffic signals. And there are rules we have to follow to keep boat traffic moving safely. To get where we want to go, we use navigational charts, which are maps of the water and shoreline. Some boaters also use a GPS (Global Positioning System) device that receives signals from satellites above the earth to compute their boat's location. But I like looking at the charts, and Mom and Dad showed me how they use them to map out our course.

Navigational charts are maps for boaters. They show latitude and longitude lines, water depths (called soundings), locations of buoys and their type (like "nun" and "can" which refer to their shape), location and depth of underwater obstacles (like shipwrecks and submerged rocks), and lots of other information that boaters need. A navigational chart also has a special kind of compass rose that is used to lay out a course to a destination. The compass rose shows a 360-degree circle with north at 0. The skipper draws lines on the chart to mark the course, then draws parallel lines on the compass rose. The lines on the compass rose show the exact compass readings the skipper must follow.

1. Look at the navigational chart on the next page. The numbers in the water are soundings, which show the water depth in feet. The lines connecting the soundings are called contour lines. Contour lines show the shape of the bottom of the lake by connecting areas of the same depth. Find Whiskey Island. What do you think it means when the contour lines are close together like they are on the southeast side of the island?

2. Look at the compass rose on the chart. The line drawn on it points to about what degree?

Using the legend, find and circle examples of the following:

3. **A shipwreck above the water, a sunken wreck, and a submerged wreck** How far below the surface is the submerged wreck?

4. **Soundings** What would a skipper use these for?

5. **A buoy** What color and type is it?

6. **A swampy area**

7. **A rocky area**

TRICKY TRIP
Captain Cornelius wants to travel from Whiskey Island to Garden Island. He has a 25-foot boat with a draft of about 4 feet. (Draft=how much of the boat is below the water line.) With a red pen and a ruler, draw a line on the chart from the eastern tip of Whiskey Island to the star on Garden Island. The captain wants to anchor at the X to do some fishing. Do you see any problems with his course?

MAKE A SOUNDINGS CHART!
Put aquarium gravel in the bottom of a container like an aquarium or deep baking pan. Give the gravel hills and valleys. Add water to make your own lake. Make a map of your lake and write in soundings that you find by measuring the water depth at different points with a ruler. Connect areas of the same depth to make contour lines.

WHY ARE DEPTH MEASUREMENTS CALLED SOUNDINGS? DOES IT HAVE ANYTHING TO DO WITH NOISE? LOOK UP THE VERB SOUND AND THE NOUN SOUNDING IN THE DICTIONARY AND FIND OUT.

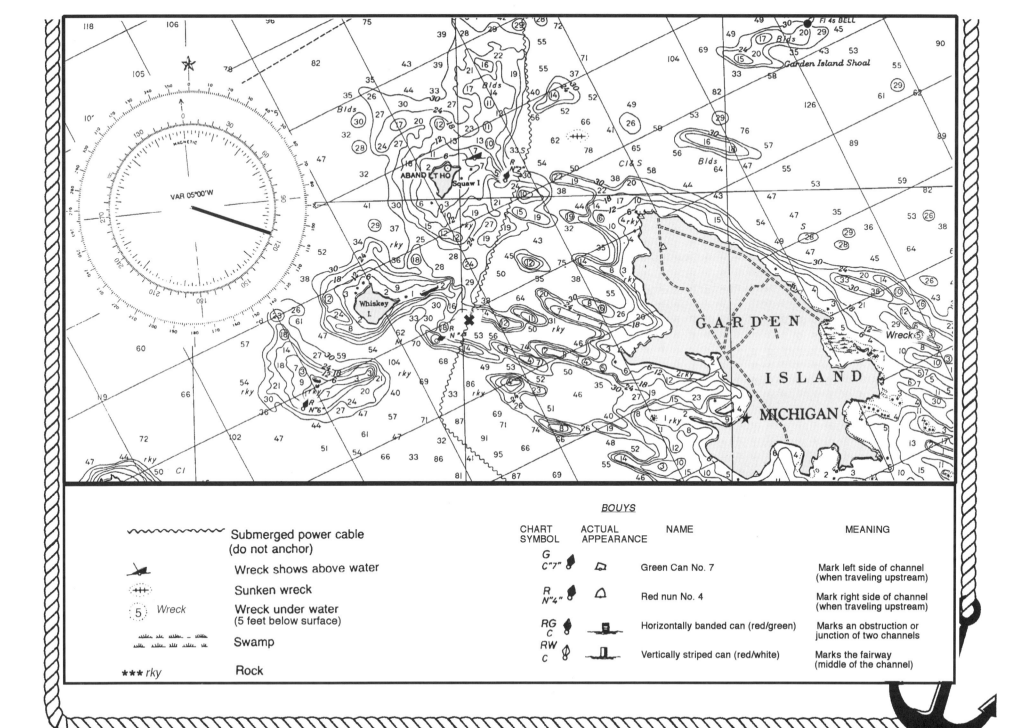

BOUYS

CHART SYMBOL	ACTUAL APPEARANCE	NAME	MEANING
G C"7"		Green Can No. 7	Mark left side of channel (when traveling upstream)
R N"4"		Red nun No. 4	Mark right side of channel (when traveling upstream)
RG C		Horizontally banded can (red/green)	Marks an obstruction or junction of two channels
RW C		Vertically striped can (red/white)	Marks the fairway (middle of the channel)

Submerged power cable (do not anchor)

Wreck shows above water

Sunken wreck

Wreck — Wreck under water (5 feet below surface)

Swamp

rky — Rock

Shipwrecks on the Inland Seas

After visiting the Great Lakes Shipwreck Museum at Whitefish Point, Michigan, I'm nervous about sailing. My parents said I shouldn't worry because most shipwrecks happen during November storms. Plus, the new computerized navigation systems, radios, accurate charts, weather forecasting, and lighthouses have made sailing on the Great Lakes a lot safer.

THE GREAT STORMS OF NOVEMBER

Captains know they must sail the Great Lakes with caution and respect. Storms here can be more dangerous than ocean storms. This is especially true in November when cold arctic air swoops down and swirls with warm air to create gale force storms. But captains also want to get in one last trip before the shipping lanes freeze up and are closed, and sometimes they have been caught in sudden and dangerous November gales. A November 1913 storm sank ten ships and threw twenty more up onto the shore. Two hundred thirty-five mariners died. Another November storm sank five ships and killed 58 men in 1940.

SHIPWRECK STORY LISTENING ACTIVITY

Listen to one of the shipwreck stories on the CD-ROM and write a newspaper article about it. For help writing your article, answer as many of the questions on the right as you can and use the information in your article.

WHO is the story about?
WHAT happened?
WHERE did it happen?
WHEN did it happen?
WHY did it happen?

SHIPWRECK PRESERVES

When men sailed the Great Lakes in wooden vessels with only a compass to guide them, shipwrecks were common. Records show nearly 3,000 shipwrecks on the Great Lakes between 1878 and 1888. Some people believe there have been over 10,000 shipwrecks in the Great Lakes. Certain areas have many shipwrecks because of shoals or other conditions that cause wrecks. Preserves have been created in some of these places. Over 80 shipwrecks are in the Bottomland Preserve of Thunder Bay, Lake Huron. People are allowed to scuba dive to the wrecks in this preserve.

FAMOUS GREAT LAKES FREIGHTER WRECKS

Freighter	Date of Sinking	Location	Survivors	Dead
Daniel J. Morrell	November 29, 1906	Saginaw Bay, Lake Huron	1	28
Charles S. Price	November 9, 1913	Southern tip of Lake Huron	0	Unknown
Carl D. Bradley	November 18, 1958	Upper Lake Michigan	2	33
Edmund Fitzgerald	November 10, 1975	Whitefish Point, Lake Superior	0	29

THE GREAT LAKES TRIANGLE: FACT OR FICTION?

Many boats and aircraft have disappeared mysteriously in the Great Lakes. A map of the incidents makes a triangle similiar to the infamous Bermuda Triangle. The Federal Aviation Administration has a special "Lake Reporting Service" because of all the odd occurences in the area. Pilots flying over the lakes must report in continuously to ground stations. If they are ten minutes late in reporting, a search and rescue operation begins. To learn more read *The Great Lakes Triangle* by Jay Gourley.

MAP ACTIVITY

Use the chart above and the legend on your Activity Map to find and label the shipwrecks of the *Morrell*, *Bradley*, *Price*, and *Fitzgerald* on the map. Label the Thunder Bay Bottomland Preserve on the map.

THE WORST DISASTER ON THE GREAT LAKES IN TERMS OF LOSS OF LIFE WASN'T DUE TO A STORM. IN 1915 THE EASTLAND CAPSIZED AT ITS DOCK IN CHICAGO KILLING OVER 800 PEOPLE.

Semper Paratus! The U.S. Coast Guard on the Great Lakes

Always ready! That's the Coast Guard's motto and it's true! They are always ready to protect property, enforce laws, and even save lives. We're in Grand Haven, Michigan, also known as Coast Guard City USA, for the annual Coast Guard Festival. I got to tour some of the big ice-breaking and buoy-tending "cutters" (that's Coast Guard talk for "ships") and learn about the important things the Coast Guard does on the Great Lakes.

The U.S. Coast Guard is the smallest of the five armed services of the United States. It was formed in 1915 when the U.S. Revenue Cutter Service and the U.S. Lifesaving Service merged. Its duties on the nation's coasts and waterways include national security, protecting our environment, search and rescue, and making sure boaters obey the laws and operate safely.

The Coast Guard is also responsible for icebreaking and taking care of navigational aids, like buoys and lighthouses. These jobs are important, because they keep the traffic moving safely on the Great Lakes. Buoys, beacons, and channel markers tell boats where to go, and where not to go. Late in the fall before the lakes freeze over, Coast Guard cutters called buoy tenders retrieve about 1,200 buoys from the Great Lakes, sometimes putting special winter buoys in their place. The buoys are repaired and stored over the winter. Then the buoy tenders put them back at winter's end to assist the next season's shipping. Besides directing traffic, special buoys measure wind speed, barometric pressure, and air temperature for weather forecasters; others measure wave height and surface conditions.

Some of the Coast Guard cutters are designed to break through winter lake ice and keep shipping lanes open as long as possible. These icebreakers can break through ice that is five feet thick!

Rocky shores, sudden storms, and dense fog have always been a threat to Great Lakes boaters. In the 1870s, lifesaving stations were set up along the shores of the Great Lakes to rescue shipwreck victims. At first these stations had 26-foot surfboats that were launched from the beach. They carried six to eight brave oarsmen and the station keeper out into danagerous waters to try to rescue survivors. Over the years lifeboats were improved, but the business of lifesaving remained a dangerous job.

Sometimes it was not necessary to send a boat out into the stormy waves to perform a rescue. If a ship were within 600 yards from shore, a "breeches buoy" could be used. This device was invented in the 1840s and was still being used in the 1950s. A line was rigged from the shore to the stranded ship and a special life ring was suspended from the line. A canvas sling, like a pair of breeches, was attached to the life ring. One at a time, people could be pulled along the line to safety, seated in the breeches buoy. Lifesaving crews had to be able to set up the breeches buoy in five minutes or less, so they practiced it every day and often had competitions among the stations.

These days the Coast Guard has more modern equipment, like helicopters, and saves over 4,000 lives each year. But when it comes to lifesaving, bravery is still the main requirement.

READY, SET, RECALL! How many things can you remember about the Coast Guard after reading the paragraphs one time? After reading two times? Test your recall with these questions:

List five things the Coast Guard does.   What is a breeches bouy and how did it get its name?   List three functions of buoys.
What are three Great Lakes shipping hazards?   How many lives does the Coast Guard save each year?

IMAGINE THAT YOU ARE WORKING ON BOARD A COAST GUARD ICEBREAKER IN THE GREAT LAKES. WHAT IS YOUR JOB LIKE? WHERE DO YOU GO? IS IT EXCITING? DANGEROUS? COLD? TELL ME ABOUT IT.

Waterway to the World: Great Lakes Commercial Shipping

Today we visited Canal Park in Duluth, Minnesota, where we watched huge freighters come and go. Duluth is the busiest port on the Great Lakes. Most of the freighters stopping here are American or Canadian, but there are plenty of ships from other countries that make their way up the St. Lawrence Seaway to Great Lakes ports. Food, machinery, coal...all kinds of stuff travels on the Great Lakes on its way across the country or around the world!

Freighters can carry huge loads and use much less fuel than either trucks or trains. This makes them the cheapest way to transport bulk cargo. Sometimes freighters on the Great Lakes work in combination with trains and trucks to deliver cargo. For example, there are no coal mines near any of the Great Lakes ports. So coal for steel mills or power plants is brought from Montana to Lake Superior by train. There it is loaded onto freighters and shipped to ports along the lakes where it may be used, or sent on to other parts of the country by train or truck. It might also be shipped to other parts of the world through the St. Lawrence Seaway.

The American freighters that carry cargo on the Great Lakes are called "lakers." There are more than 70 "U.S.-flag" lakers, or freighters registered in the U.S. Thirteen of them are 1,000 footers. Almost all the American lakers are self-unloading, which means that they have built-in equipment for unloading their cargo. The self-unloader is a Great Lakes invention. A 1,000-foot laker can unload 70,000 tons of coal in less than 10 hours without any outside help or equipment. Lakers can be used to carry lots of different kinds of cargo, so a freighter can carry iron ore to one place, then load up with coal for the return trip. Only liquid bulk cargoes and cement need special kinds of boats built just for them. The biggest cargo carried by U.S. freighters on the Great Lakes is iron ore— more than 61 million tons each season! The next biggest are limestone and coal.

In 1920 Congress passed the Jones Act, or the Merchant Marine Act, which says that all ships that load cargo at one U.S. port and unload it at another U.S. port must be built in America, registered in America, and have an American crew.

A 1,000 foot laker can carry 70,000 tons of coal. A truck can carry 60 tons. A rail car can carry 120 tons.
1. How many trucks would it take to carry the load of one 1,000-foot laker?   2. How many rail cars?

Re-read the information above about the Jones Act and think about why our government cares who builds, owns, and runs the ships that carry cargo between Great Lakes ports.
3. How do you think the Jones Act might make shipping safer on the Great Lakes?

CARGO SHIPS IN THE GREAT LAKES ARE "DOWNBOUND" WHEN HEADING TOWARD THE SEA AND "UPBOUND" WHEN HEADING INLAND. IN LAKE MICHIGAN, EITHER DIRECTION CAN BE UPBOUND, DEPENDING ON THE SHIP'S DESTINATION.

Ship Watching on the Great Lakes

When we're out on the lakes, we see all kinds of boats: little speed boats, sailboats, tugs and dredges, buoy tenders, and fishing boats. But my mom and dad are really good at identifying all the different types of freighters. Here's everything I've learned about them, so when you're on the lakes, you can tell them apart.

Most of the cargo carriers on the Great Lakes are owned by Canadian or American shipping companies. But Great Lakes ports also receive ships from more than 60 different countries each year. Freighters carry general or bulk cargo. General cargo might be anything from machinery to packaged food. Bulk cargoes are things that are not in containers—like coal or grain—and are loaded directly into special bulk cargo holds in the ship. Bulk cargoes may also be liquid. Some bulk cargo ships are self-unloaders, meaning they have a special conveyor belt on a boom attached to their decks to mechanically unload the cargo.

Cargo ships on the Great Lakes range from 500 to 1,000 feet in length. The Soo Locks can handle ships up to 1,100 feet in length, but locks in the St. Lawrence Seaway can only take ships up to 740 feet. So the largest freighters on the lakes are lake-bound, too big to travel to the ocean.

Here are some things to look for when you are ship watching:

♦ The **ship's name** is on the bow and the stern.

♦ **Draft marks** on the ship's bow show how deep the ship is sitting in the water.

♦ **Plimsoll markings** on the sides of the ship show how deep the ship can be loaded in all kinds of water conditions. They look something like this. ☞

♦ On the stern, below the ship's name, is its **port of registry.**

♦ Ships fly the **flag** of their home country at their stern, and sometimes the flag of the country they are visiting at their bow.

♦ The **fleet insignia** of the company that owns the ship is usually on the smoke stack.

♦ The **self-unloading boom** on the big freighters is usually about 250 feet long. You can use it to estimate a ship's length from a distance: a 1,000-foot freighter is about four boom-lengths long.

LR: Lloyd's Registry
TF: Tropical Fresh Water
F: Fresh Water
T: Tropical
S: Summer
W: Winter
WNA: Winter North Atlantic

DRAW LINES TO CONNECT THESE SHIPS WITH THEIR DESCRIPTIONS.

Ocean Bulk Freighter: *500-700 feet in length, it can carry up to 1 million bushels of grain, or general cargo. You can see its flat deck and its wheelhouse at the back end ("aft").*

Ocean General Cargo Vessel: *500-730 feet long, it has several derricks and booms above deck for loading and unloading various kinds of general cargo. It can also carry bulk cargo, up to 20,000 tons.*

Lakes Bulk Freighter: *600-800 feet long, it carries 30,000 tons of dry bulk cargo. You can see the hatch covers along the deck, but no self-unloading boom. Its wheelhouse is at the front end ("forword").*

Self-Unloading Laker: *500-1,000 feet long, the largest have cargo capacity over 70,000 tons. You can see the self-unloading boom.*

IF YOU OWNED A GREAT LAKES SHIPPING COMPANY, WHAT WOULD THE SHIPS IN YOUR FLEET LOOK LIKE? WHAT WOULD THEY CARRY? WHAT WOULD YOUR COMPANY LOGO LOOK LIKE? DRAW ME A PICTURE OF ONE OF YOUR SHIPS.

Ship Ahoy! Signal Flags and Other Codes

Today I saw some boats with colorful flags on their rigging. My mom said the flags are used to send messages, but how can flags say anything?

These nautical signal flags represent letters of the alphabet. Ships used to string them together on their rigging to send messages to other ships. Flags are still used to convey information, even though ships can now communicate with radios. Each of these alphabet flags has been assigned a special meaning, for example the A or "Alpha" flag means "diver down" and the B or "Bravo" flag means "dangerous cargo."

INVENT YOUR OWN ALPHABET CODE! USE A DIFFERENT SYMBOL FOR EACH LETTER OF THE ALPHABET. SHARE YOUR CODE WITH A FRIEND AND SEND SECRET MESSAGES.

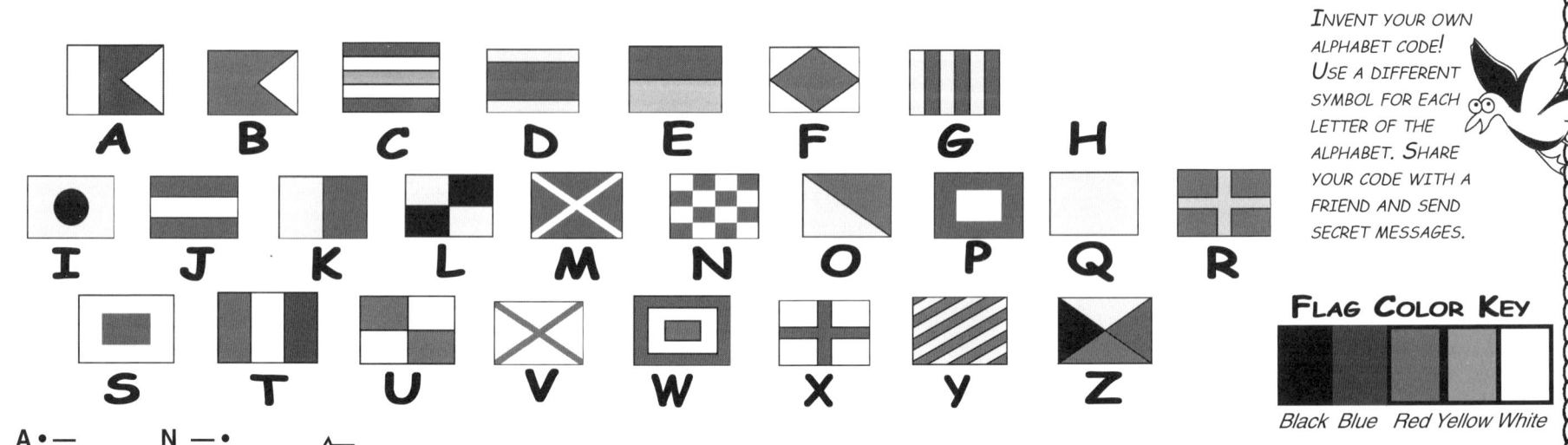

FLAG COLOR KEY

Black Blue Red Yellow White

A •—	N —•
B —•••	O ———
C —•—•	P •——•
D —••	Q ——•—
E •	R •—•
F ••—•	S •••
G ——•	T —
H ••••	U ••—
I ••	V •••—
J •———	W •——
K —•—	X —••—
L •—••	Y —•——
M ——	Z ——••

Have you seen this code before? It's Morse code, invented in the 1800s by Samuel Morse. He developed the telegraph, for sending messages electronically, and this is the alphabet code it used. The dots are short sounds and the dashes are longer sounds. You can also send messages in Morse code with a flashlight, using short flashes for the dots and longer ones for the dashes.

THINK ABOUT IT! Both of these codes were invented for communication between people who are too far apart to talk to each other. The signal flag code has to be seen to be understood; Morse code can be seen or heard. There are many different types of codes. Braille is a code that is read by touch.

1. Think carefully about how codes work and then write your own definition of what a code is.

2. Codes are not languages. Can you think of some ways that codes and languages are different?

ACTIVITY: MAKE YOUR NAME IN FLAGS

Make each letter of your name on a sheet of paper. Tack both ends of a piece of yarn or string horizontally on your wall and hang up your name. What are some shortcomings of using signal flags to communicate?

Lighting the Way

I love going inside old lighthouses, and there are lots of them around the Great Lakes. Today we went past Marblehead Lighthouse on the southwest shore of Lake Erie. It was built in 1821 and is the oldest active lighthouse on the Great Lakes. Here's everything I've learned about lighthouses so far:

By the middle of the 1800s, there were many lighthouses on the Great Lakes. Most of them had modern "Fresnel" (fray-nel) lenses that could be seen up to 20 miles away. The light was produced by an oil flame (later, electric bulbs), and the lens concentrated and intensifed its beam with an arrangement of prisms around a center magnifying glass. Lighthouse lights were colored or white, constant (fixed), rotating, or flashing. Lights along a coast each had different characteristics so that mariners would know which was which.

The lighthouse keeper had to clean the inside and outside of the storm panes, the lens, and the lamp chimney, and always have extra lamps and chimneys ready. The clockwork mechanism of rotating lights had to be wound, cleaned, and oiled regularly. All the daily lighthouse maintenance had to be completed by 10:00 a.m. each day. During the night the keeper kept the light burning by carefully trimming the lamp wicks, adjusting the vents, and winding the clockworks. Today lighthouses are unmanned and contain computerized equipment to analyze the weather, activate fog signals, and send radar signals to passing ships.

Pick a Topic!

THERE ARE LOTS OF INTERESTING STORIES ABOUT GREAT LAKES LIGHTHOUSES. RESEARCH AND WRITE ABOUT ONE THAT YOU FIND, OR PICK ONE OF THESE: THE DIFFICULT CONSTRUCTION OF SPLIT ROCK LIGHTHOUSE IN MINNESOTA; THE STORMY NIGHT IN 1838 WHEN THE BOIS BLANC LIGHT IN LAKE HURON COLLAPSED (BUT NOT BEFORE THE KEEPER'S SISTER RESCUED ITS PRECIOUS LAMP AND LENS); THE UNUSUAL FEATURE OF BARCELONA LIGHTHOUSE IN LAKE ERIE THAT MADE IT THE ONLY ONE OF ITS KIND IN THE WORLD; THE INVENTION AND DESIGN OF THE FRESNEL LENS; OR THE USE OF LIGHTSHIPS.

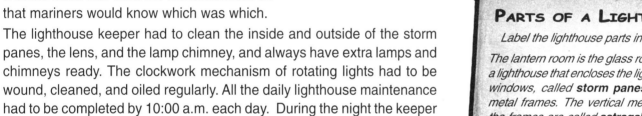

PARTS OF A LIGHTHOUSE

Label the lighthouse parts in bold below:

The lantern room is the glass room on top of a lighthouse that encloses the light. The glass windows, called **storm panes**, are set in metal frames. The vertical metal pieces of the frames are called **astragals**. There are **hand holds** on the astragals for the keeper to hold on to when cleaning the outside of the storm panes. The **lens** is inside the lantern room, and the lamp is the light source inside the lens. Around the outside of the lantern room is a balcony called a **gallery** where the keeper goes to clean and maintain the outside of the lantern room. Below the lantern room is the **service room** where the machinery for rotating the lens is located, as well as fuel tanks and vents. Above the lantern room is a **dome** roof with a special **ball vent** on top to pull air up from floor vents and prevent fogging of the storm panes. On top of the vent is a **lightning rod**.

MAP ACTIVITY

Which Great Lakes lighthouse is closest to you? Mark it on your Great Lakes Activity Map with a circle and label it. Mark any other lighthouse locations you know of on the Map. Add the lighthouse symbol to your legend.

Locks and Canals

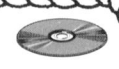

The Great Lakes are like one big river carrying people and cargo all over the Midwest! But before Americans started building canals, like the Erie Canal in the early 1800s, ships couldn't travel the Great Lakes like they can today. The connecting rivers were full of rapids and waterfalls that boats couldn't pass through. Canals turned the Great Lakes into a water highway!

Canals were built to carry boats around obstacles or to connect bodies of water. In some places canals contain locks that work like big water elevators to lift or lower ships to a different elevation. Canals connected towns to the Great Lakes, or to rivers that flow into the Great Lakes, so that people could travel throughout the region on the water. (There weren't many roads in the early 1800s, and the few that existed were pretty bad.) Opening up the Great Lakes region to shipping meant lots more people moving in and lots of new businesses. Farmers in Ohio could sell their goods in New York City. Iron ore and copper could be mined in northern Michigan and shipped to the cities in the East. Immigrants could make their new homes all around the Great Lakes area.

The **Erie Canal** was in use from 1825 through the early part of the 20th century. By that time railroads and better roads took its place.

In Canada, the **Welland Canal** carries boats around Niagara Falls, between Lake Erie and Lake Ontario.

The **Soo Canals and Soo Locks** allow boats to navigate around the rapids of the St. Marys River at Sault Ste. Marie, Michigan, connecting Lake Superior and Lake Huron.

The huge **St. Lawrence Seaway** Project, completed in 1959, created a waterway from Montreal to Lake Erie deep enough for ocean ships to enter the Great Lakes. It was a giant project, since highways, railroads, bridges, and entire towns had to be moved.

Dig these canals!

1. Why are the locks and canals of the Great Lakes and the St. Lawrence Seaway important?

2. Why did the population of Michigan and Ohio grow so fast in the mid-1800s?

3. Why are the oldest towns in Michigan along the lake shores and not in the middle of the state?

MAP ACTIVITY

Locate and label the Soo Locks (11D) and the Welland Canal (16H) on your Great Lakes Activity Map.

Hoggees, Hayburners, and Hoodledashers

Today we visited the Erie Canal Museum in Syracuse, New York. It's in a neat old "weighlock" building where they used to weigh the canal boats that came right through it. I learned a lot about the Erie Canal, the people who built it, and the people who used it.

The Erie Canal connected Lake Erie to the Hudson River in New York. It took eight years of digging through forests, swamps, and mountains to build it. When it was finished, it was 363 miles long, 40 feet wide, four feet deep, and contained 83 locks and several aqueducts. Nothing like it had ever been built in America. Without dynamite or modern equipment, men dug the canal by hand and with teams of horses hitched to special plows and scrapers.

When the Erie Canal opened in 1825 it caused many changes. Immigrants could now travel west to make their new homes in places that had been hard to get to. Farmers in the Midwest could sell their grain and produce in far-away New York. And new towns sprang up all along the canal. Canal boats were pulled by mules, and boys as young as 12 years old were hired to drive the mules along the towpath next to the canal. These boys were nicknamed **hoggees** and the mules were sometimes called **hayburners** or **long-eared robins**.

Many different kinds of boats used the Erie Canal. Freight boats were called **bullheads**. Fancy passenger boats were **packets**, while slower passenger boats were called **line boats**. A **hoodledasher** was a full cargo boat that was towing two or more empty boats. When the canal needed quick repairs for leaks or bank erosion, a repair scow, or **hurry-up boat**, was called. Boats traveling the Erie Canal had to obey a speed limit of four miles per hour. This was mainly to prevent waves that would erode the banks of the canal.

The Erie Canal opened the Midwest to immigration and commerce, but by the early 1900s railroads took over the work the Erie Canal had done. In 1918 the wider, deeper New York State Barge Canal was completed, and still exists. Other canals, like the Welland Canal connecting Lake Ontario and Lake Erie, are important shipping routes today.

1. If you stood in the Erie Canal when it was first built, how much of you would be above the water?

2. Look up **aqueduct** in the dictionary. Then draw a picture of one on a separate sheet of paper and describe how it works.

3. Look at a map of your state and find its scale. If you started digging a canal the length of the Erie Canal in your town, where would it end?

MAP ACTIVITY

On your Great Lakes Activity Map, draw a green line representing the Erie Canal. Start at Albany, NY. Follow the Mohawk River, then cut across north of the Finger Lakes to Buffalo, NY. Add the green line to your map's legend.

CANAL FACTS: TOURISTS FROM ALL OVER THE WORLD PAID ABOUT $.04 A MILE TO CRUISE THE CANAL ON PACKETS CARRYING 40 TO 100 PASSENGERS. THE ENTIRE TRIP TOOK ABOUT SIX DAYS. BEFORE THE CANAL, SHIPPING GOODS FROM BUFFALO TO NEW YORK COST ABOUT $100 A TON; ON THE CANAL IT COST BETWEEN $4 AND $12 A TON. THE CANAL HAD SEVEN WEIGHLOCKS TO WEIGH THE BOATS AND COLLECT TOLLS. BY 1883 MORE THAN $121 MILLION HAD BEEN COLLECTED, COVERING CONSTRUCTION COSTS, REPAIRS, OPERATION, AND ENLARGEMENT OF THE CANAL. TOLLS WERE THEN ABOLISHED.

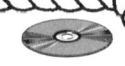

How Does a Lock Work?

Today we stopped in Sault Ste. Marie, Michigan, and went in the information center at the Soo Locks. The St. Marys River connects Lake Superior and Lake Huron here. But until the locks were built in 1855, ships couldn't navigate it because of dangerous rapids that drop about 20 feet from Superior to Huron. Now a canal takes ships around the rapids, and locks raise and lower them, just like an elevator. At the information center I saw a model of how the locks work.

Locks are like elevators for ships. Each lock has walls on the sides and watertight gates at the front and back. To lower a ship, the water inside the lock is brought up to the level of the upstream side, where the ship is waiting. Then one set of gates is opened and a panel of signal lights tells the ship it may enter the lock. The gates are closed behind it. Water is let out of the lock to lower the ship to the level of the downstream side. The front gates are opened and the ship leaves the lock. Locks raise ships the same way, letting water into the lock until it is the right level. No pumps are used to move water in and out of a lock, just gravity. Special valves are opened on the upstream side of the lock to let water flow in to raise the level; other valves can be opened toward the downstream side to let water flow out of the lock. The locks that carry ships around Niagara Falls and through the St. Lawrence Seaway work the same way.

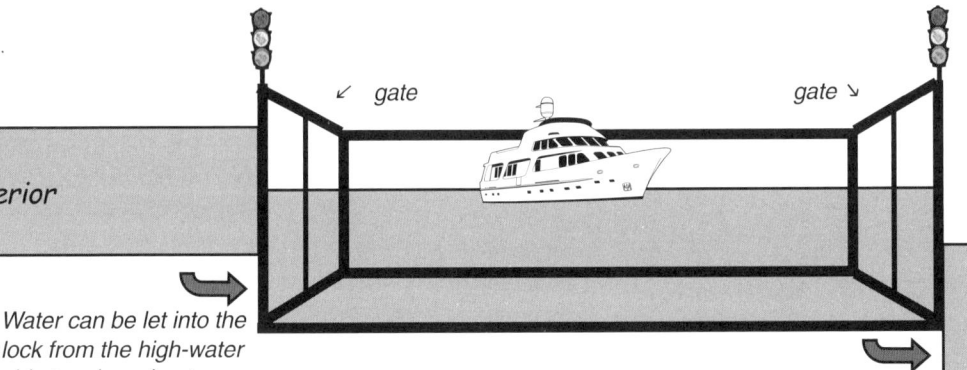

gate ↙   gate ↘

⇦ to Lake Superior

to Lake Huron ⇨

Water can be let into the lock from the high-water side to raise a boat.

Water can be let out of the lock into the low-water side to lower a boat.

PILOT YOUR FREIGHTER THROUGH A LOCK!

You want to travel from Lake Huron to Lake Superior through the Soo Locks. Number the following steps to show how your freighter is lifted up by the locks.

_____Special valves let water into your lock from the upstream side, raising your freighter up.

_____You approach the lock and wait for the lock signal lights to tell you when to enter.

_____The entrance gates close behind you. The exit gates in front of you remain closed, making the lock a watertight chamber.

_____Now the water in your lock is at the same level as the upstream side. The gates in front of you open and you steer out of the lock.

_____The entrance gates of the lock open and you steer your freighter into the lock.

BEFORE THE LOCKS WERE BUILT AT SAULT STE. MARIE, SHIPS HAD TO PORTAGE AROUND THE FALLS IN THE ST. MARYS RIVER. THE SHIPS WERE UNLOADED, DRAGGED AROUND THE FALLS ON GREASED LOGS OR ROLLERS BY MULES, THEN RELOADED.

Mighty Mac

Today we went through the Straits of Mackinac, which connect Lake Michigan and Lake Huron. We went under the Mackinac Bridge, one of the largest suspension bridges in the world! It's huge! How did people ever build something so big? And how do they take care of it? Before it was built, I wonder if the people in Michigan's two peninsulas ever got to see each other?

THE MACKINAC BRIDGE, which took three and a half years to build, was completed in 1957. Before that, people crossed the Straits by boat or on the ice in winter. Cars often waited in long lines to board car ferries. During deer hunting season, the wait was sometimes up to eight and a half hours! Gas stations along the road had pumps with extra-long hoses to reach the cars as they waited in line, and vendors went car to car selling snacks. In the winter, cars drove across the ice. The whole bridge, including its approaches, is about five miles long. It had to be made to withstand high winds and storms, the severe climate at the Straits, and the weight of many vehicles, so it's strong but flexible. Its two giant towers are 552 feet tall and they bend toward or away from each other as much as 18 feet depending on the weight of vehicles on the bridge. On windy days, the bridge bows out to the side as much as 20 feet! Temperature affects it, too. It moves up and down as much as 12 feet depending on the temperature—about one inch per degree. Maintenance is a never-ending job on such a huge structure. It takes about nine years to paint the entire bridge and uses about 70,000 gallons of paint!

HOW BIG IS IT?

1. Measure the wall of your bedroom or classroom from the floor to the ceiling. The towers of the Mackinac Bridge are 552 feet tall from the waterline. How many of your rooms would you have to stack up to make 552 feet?

2. Now measure the floor of your room from one wall to the opposite wall. The main span (tower to tower) of the Mackinac Bridge is 3,800 feet. How many of your rooms would you have to line up to make 3,800 feet?

   How many football fields make 3,800 feet?

3. The Mackinac Bridge is about five miles long, including the approaches on either end of the main span. Name something that is about five miles from your home or school.

MAP ACTIVITY

On your Great Lakes Activity Map, show the location of the Mackinac Bridge and label it.

HAVE YOU EVER CROSSED THE MACKINAC BRIDGE OR ANOTHER BIG BRIDGE? WRITE ME A STORY ABOUT CROSSING A BIG BRIDGE. IT CAN BE REAL OR MADE-UP.

Great Lakes Tourism Then and Now

What? I could hardly believe my parents when they told me people had been playing in and along the Great Lakes for more than a century—like forever. Mom showed me old pictures of people at the beach. The women were in outfits that look like dresses and the men wore one-piece long underwear. Pretty weird! Thinking about all those people from my history books in those crazy bathing suits was a good way to keep from being bored.

Read each of the following sentences and decide if it describes the Great Lakes activities in the 1880s, the 2000s, or both times. Write a **T** (then), **N** (now) or **B** (both) in the space provided.

_____ 1. People from Chicago, St. Louis, and Detroit travel by steamboats and trains to spend their summers at cottages and resorts along the Great Lakes.

_____ 2. Mackinac Island, between Lake Michigan and Lake Huron, draws large numbers of tourists each summer.

_____ 3. People rent swim suits and slide on large slides into the lake.

_____ 4. Sailing is popular on the Great Lakes.

_____ 5. Jet skis and large racing boats are popular on the Great Lakes.

_____ 6. Thousands visit Niagara Falls and ride on tour boats that take them close to the base of the falls.

_____ 7. People camp along the Great Lakes and go fishing there.

_____ 8. Ferry boats take people to various islands in the Great Lakes.

_____ 9. Wagons carry people and their trunks from the steamship landings to cottages and resorts.

_____ 10. Many people tour the Great Lakes by driving around them in their automobiles.

_____ 11. Cruise ships where people dine, dance, and enjoy the scenery can be found on the lakes.

_____ 12. People fish for Pacific salmon in Lake Michigan.

_____ 13. Tourists have a choice of hundreds of recreational places and attractions along the Great Lakes.

_____ 14. Only a few towns and parks along the lakes attract tourists.

_____ 15. The only true wilderness areas left around the Great Lakes are along the northern shores of Lake Superior and Lake Huron.

Going Places in the Great Lakes

Dad says tourism is a big business in the Great Lakes states. When people visit a place, they spend money on gas, food, and other stuff—my personal favorite is T-shirts. The more visitors that come, the more money businesses make.

Think of a tourist attraction or popular place you have visited in the Great Lakes region and answer the questions.

1. Where did you go?

2. Why did you go there?

3. How did you get there? How much did it cost to travel there (gasoline costs, air fare, etc.)?

4. What did you do or see?

5. How many meals did you eat there? How much did you spend?

6. Did you stay overnight? Where? How much did it cost?

7. What souvenirs did you buy? How much did they cost?

8. Put a check by the businesses and services below that earn extra money when tourists arrive in their town.

____ schools	____ gift shops	____ factories	____ museums
____ restaurants	____ golf courses	____ hotels & motels	____ dentists
____ ice cream stands	____ gas stations	____ fruit farms	____ grocery stores

YOU OWN A GREAT LAKES CRUISE SHIP COMPANY. WHICH PORTS WILL YOU TAKE YOUR PASSENGERS TO? WHY? DESIGN A BROCHURE ADVERTISING YOUR COMPANY'S CRUISES.

BE AN ENTREPRENEUR!

People who start businesses are called entrepreneurs (on-tru-pre-nurs). Imagine you live in a town along one of the Great Lakes and you want to start a business. What kind of business would you start that might attract tourists? Why? Could you still earn money from the business at times during the year when there were few or no tourists? If yes, explain why your business could still operate. If no, what would you do to earn money until the next tourist season?

Falling for Niagara Falls

Niagara Falls is awesome! The waterfalls are made by the Niagara River going down a huge cliff. There is an island right at the top that splits the river before it reaches the edge to make two waterfalls. People come from all over the world to the falls. I heard lots of languages. It's funny that people just stand and stare at the falls for such a long time. I wonder why we are so attracted to them?

People have been drawn to the falls at Niagara for centuries. The spectacle of 150,000 gallons of water per minute plunging 182 feet has inspired sacrifices, poetry, and dangerous stunts.

The Indians thought they heard the voice of the Great Spirit in the thunderous falls. Each spring they chose a girl of the tribe to paddle a white canoe over the edge as a human sacrifice to the Great Spirit. The maiden chosen considered it a great honor.

By 1820 the falls were becoming a tourist attraction. To draw larger crowds (and more guests), the local hotel owners arranged to send an old schooner loaded with animals over the falls. Advertisements said that the boat would be loaded with "ferocious creatures" such as panthers and wolves. But when the boat launched, it carried only a buffalo, two small bears, two racoons, a dog, and a goose. The schooner broke up before reaching the falls and the bears swam to shore. The other animals went down the waterfall. Only the goose survived the trip.

Tourist crowds grew and the stunts continued. People went over the falls in barrels, walked tightropes, dove into the rapids and performed many other stunts. One man tied an iron anvil to his feet before plummeting over the falls in a barrel. The anvil broke through the bottom of the barrel and pulled him along. Only his right arm was still strapped in when the barrel was recovered. Stunts were outlawed in 1912, but daredevils continued to challenge the falls. Most lost the challenge and died.

MAP ACTIVITY

On your Great Lakes Activity Map, locate and label Niagara Falls (17H).

HENNEPIN VS. DICKENS

Father Hennepin visited the falls in 1678. He found their great power frightening. He wrote: "The waters which fall from this horrible precipice do boil and foam after the most hideous manner imaginable, making an outrageous noise more terrible than thunder."

Charles Dickens thought differently of the falls. He wrote: "...the first effect, and the enduring one–instant and lasting–of the tremendous spectacle was Peace. Peace of Mind, tranquility, calm recollections of the Dead, great thoughts of Eternal Rest and Happiness..."

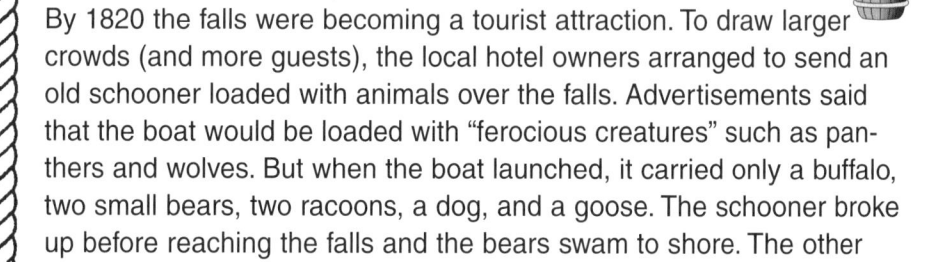

```
D E L B I R R E T Z T A O B U R A R E
A L E T E W A X T H E T I C K E I D R
R B O C B A R R E L S S S N T U S C H S
E I Q U A C T R A N Q U I L I T Y R P
D R E V E E P E O T T O U R I S T S I
E R U G E O P S S S E N I P P A H W R
V O U T R A G E O U S B E C H C A T I
I H I D E O U S A Z E P O R T H G I T
L U I J P L O T R E N B A G H P U Q U
```

WORDSEARCH

Use these clues to find the words in the wordsearch!
1. Four adjectives Hennepin used to describe the falls.
2. Today the falls attract thousands of _____ .
3. Name for a person who performs stunts.
4. Two objects people used to "challenge" the falls.
5. Four pleasant things the falls made Dickens think of (single words)
6. The Indians heard the Great _____ in the falls.

Troubling Toxins: The Story of DDT

We were fishing on Lake Michigan near Frankfort when my dad caught a huge lake trout. I was surprised when he threw it back in the water. He said that Lake Michigan lake trout over 23" have too many toxins like DDT and PCB in them, so they are dangerous to eat. He explained that toxins are poisons that get in the water and contaminate the zooplankton (tiny water creatures). Little fish eat the zooplankton and big fish eat the little fish. The toxins get passed right along. The bigger and older the fish, the more toxins it has in its body.

The story of DDT taught us much about the impact of toxins on the Great Lakes. In the 1960s DDT was sprayed on trees to prevent Dutch elm disease and was also widely used for insect control. DDT entered the lakes and contaminated the water and the zooplankton. Soon DDT began to move up the food chain to the fish and birds. Fish and birds collected the toxins in their bodies, until they contained high levels of the poison. This accumulation of toxins in a living thing is called **bioaccumulation**.

Large fish and fish-eating birds at the top of the food chain were found to have levels of DDT thousands of times higher than the concentrations in the lake water. The concentration of the toxin was increasing with each step of the food chain. This process is called **biomagnification**.

High concentrations of DDT caused birth defects, cancer, and death. DDT also caused the shells of falcon eggs to be too thin. The eggs broke under the weight of the nesting parents. This severely reduced the falcon population during the 1970s. People learned many hard lessons about toxins from DDT.

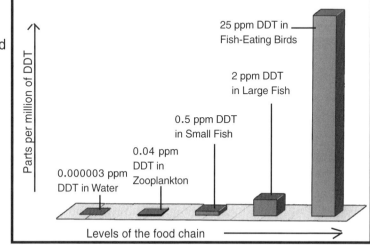

Chart — *Parts per million of DDT* (vertical axis) vs *Levels of the food chain* (horizontal axis):
- 0.000003 ppm DDT in Water
- 0.04 ppm DDT in Zooplankton
- 0.5 ppm DDT in Small Fish
- 2 ppm DDT in Large Fish
- 25 ppm DDT in Fish-Eating Birds

1. According to the chart, which would be safer to eat: three small fish that feed on zooplankton, or one large fish that feeds on small fish? Why?

2. An increase in the concentration of toxins in a living thing over time is called _____ .

3. An increase in the concentration of toxins in living things with each step of the food chain is called_____.

4. What are three results of high concentrations of DDT? How did DDT affect the falcon population?

5. How many times greater is the concentration of DDT in a fish-eating bird than in a small fish?

FRIGHTENING FACTS

One meal of Lake Michigan lake trout contains more PCBs than a lifetime supply of Lake Michigan drinking water.

Most pollution enters the Great Lakes from the air. Pollutants may be from sources thousands of miles away.

WHAT ARE SOME OTHER THREATS TO THE GREAT LAKES YOU HAVE READ OR HEARD ABOUT? LEARN MORE ABOUT ONE AND WRITE A PARAGRAPH ON IT.

We've Been Invaded! The Sea Lamprey

We spent the day exploring Madeline Island, Wisconsin. It used to be a fishing town, but now it's a tourist resort. We went to the Madeline Island Historical Museum and saw some neat exhibits about the island's fishing industry. Fishing used to be a big business here but was ruined in the early 1940s when sea lamprey started killing the big fish. In just a few years there weren't enough fish left to support the fishermen and their families.

In the last 200 years more than 160 species of plants, fish, and other organisms have invaded the Great Lakes. Many people first became aware of the problems these invaders could create when sea lamprey migrated to the lakes from the Atlantic Ocean. The lamprey swam up the St. Lawrence River to Lake Ontario, but Niagara Falls prevented them from traveling farther for many years. In 1919 the Welland Canal was deepened, providing lamprey with a route around Niagara Falls. By 1938 sea lamprey had spread throughout the Great Lakes.

Sea lamprey are eel-like creatures with a sucker mouth filled with sharp teeth. They attach to large fish and feed on their blood and body fluids. Most of their prey die. Before sea lamprey entered the Great Lakes, the U.S. and Canadian trout catch for Lakes Huron and Superior was 15 million pounds per year. By 1960 the catch was only 300,000 pounds per year. The fishing industry was devastated.

Today the sea lamprey population is under control thanks to joint efforts by the U.S. and Canada. A poison called TFM is used to kill lamprey larvae. Lamprey populations are also reduced by other methods which limit their reproduction.

1. How did the sea lamprey change the main industry of Madeline Island?

2. The fish catch of Lakes Huron and Superior was reduced by how many pounds per year from the early 1900s to 1960?

3. What or who do you think is responsible for the decline of the fishing industry? Why?

4. What other types of businesses can you think of that may have been affected by the loss of fish?

ORGANIZE THE INFO

Fill in the chart to organize the information in the text.

1. Origin of Sea Lamprey	*2. How sea lamprey entered the lakes.*

3. How sea lamprey harmed the Great Lakes and its people

4. Solutions to the problem

MAP ACTIVITY

Study your map. What transportation route has let in non-native species as well as cargoes from around the world? Draw a purple line along this route and add it to the legend as the "International Shipping Route."

One Thing Leads to Another: How Zebra Mussels Are Changing the Great Lakes

We anchored in a little bay to have a picnic. I was walking to shore when I stepped on a rock covered with zebra mussels and got a deep cut on my foot. My Dad put iodine on it and that hurt worse than the cut. I hate zebra mussels! I hate iodine!

Zebra mussels are striped, fingernail size mussels which entered the Great Lakes about 1986. They attach firmly to any hard surface, including each other, and form huge colonies. Beds of zebra mussels have been found which contain up to 70,000 mussels per square meter. That's 70,000 mussels in an area the size of a bathtub! Zebra mussels coat and clog the intake pipes of water and power plants and have caused a few to temporarily shut down. They get into boat engines and cause them to overheat. They sink navigation buoys with their weight. Besides being a nuisance to man, this tiny pest is changing the Great Lakes ecosystem. Study the diagram to learn more and answer the questions.

Diagram boxes:

- Zebra mussels enter the Great Lakes when ships dump ballast water from foreign places into the lakes.
- Zebra mussels spread throughout the Lakes and multiply.
- Zebra mussels eat by filtering large quantities of plankton (microscopic water plants & animals) out of the water. In some areas mussels have removed 80% of the plankton from the water.
- Small fish don't have enough to eat and die.
- Too much blue green algae grows in the filtered water.
- Through filter feeding zebra mussels accumulate 10 times more toxins than other fish.
- Too many plants start growing in the filtered water.
- Blue green algae makes drinking water taste bad.
- Sport fish eat mussels and are contaminated with toxins.
- People eat sport fish and take in toxins.

1. What **behavior** of zebra mussels is changing the water in the Great Lakes ecosystem?

2. How is this affecting the plant population in the Great Lakes?

3. What are two ways that fish are being harmed by zebra mussels?

4. List at least four ways people are affected by zebra mussels.

5. Explain how the presence of zebra mussels in the Great Lakes has led to an increase in toxins in sport fish.

Ballast Water "Unbalances" the Ecosystem

A ship not carrying cargo takes on water in special chambers to add ballast or weight to the vessel. This balances and stabilizes the ship. The ship then travels to the port where it is to be loaded and dumps the ballast water. This ballast water can contain plants and fish which are foreign to that ecosystem and have no enemies. These invaders then multiply quickly, compete for food with native species, and may even cause extinction of native species. Invaders destroy the "balance" of the ecosystem. Most ships entering the Great Lakes now dump their ballast water in the ocean to avoid introducing invaders.

Challenges Ahead

I read about the shipping of nuclear waste on Lake Michigan in the newspaper. Some people quoted in the article said it is very risky, but others said nuclear waste has been transported since 1964 without a major accident. I don't know who is right.

As we move into the future we must carefully consider the impact of our activities on the lakes. Issues such as whether or not to ship nuclear waste on the lakes are difficult ones. What could happen? What will the effect be in ten years? In 100 years? Do we have all the facts at this time? Citizens, scientists, and legislators wrestle with these issues. We have many challenges ahead as we work to keep the lakes great.

SELLING GREAT LAKES WATER

For many years entrepreneurs have been interested in removing and selling water from the Great Lakes. Occasionally dry western states have also expressed interest in importing Great Lakes water. People decided that something had to be done to protect the waters of the Great Lakes. In September of 2000 the Water Resources Development Act of 1986 was amended to ban removal of water from the lakes. In 2002 the Canadian government also proposed regulations to protect against the bulk removal of water from the Great Lakes.

DRILLING FOR OIL AND GAS UNDER THE GREAT LAKES

If you travel along the Canadian shores of Lake Erie you may see an oil or gas well near the shore. Directional or slant drilling allows wells on the shore to tap oil and gas reserves under the lake bottom. About 2,200 wells have been drilled under Lake Erie since 1913 by Canadian firms. In 1979, 13 directional wells were drilled under Lake Michigan. Michigan was the only Great Lakes state which had not banned directional drilling at that time. Concerned citizens pushed lawmakers to ban directional drilling in Michigan in 2002.

TRANSPORTING NUCLEAR WASTE ON THE GREAT LAKES

If the Yucca Mountain nuclear waste dump opens in 2010, nuclear waste from power plants in Michigan and Wisconsin could be shipped on Lake Michigan through the ports of Milwaukee and Muskegon. Supporters say the casks containing the waste won't break even in a bad accident. Critics say it's not worth the risk of contaminating the drinking water supply of millions of people.

1. On what issue did the U.S. and Canada choose different courses of action?

2. On what issue did they agree?

3. Why is it important for both the United States and Canada to support measures to protect the lakes?

4. Why is the Water Resources Development Act important? What might happen if we did not have this act?

5. Why is it so difficult for people to know if it is safe to transport nuclear waste on the Great Lakes?

6. Do you think nuclear waste should be moved on the Great Lakes? Give at least two reasons for your answer.

THINK ABOUT THINGS YOU DO OR USE WHICH MIGHT HARM THE LAKES. WHAT IS IT? WHY IS IT HARMFUL? WHAT CAN YOU DO TO PROTECT THE LAKES?

Keeping Our Lakes Great

We are staying at Fish Creek Municipal Marina on Green Bay. Some fishermen were taking their boats out of the water and were draining their bilges. When I asked why, they said it was to get rid of any zebra mussels that might have gotten into the bilge. They were going fishing on an inland lake the next day and didn't want to spread the zebra mussels.

Many people work hard to keep our lakes healthy. We can already see some of the results of their efforts. Here are just a few ways people, groups, and governments are keeping the lakes great.

- The Midwest Peregrine Falcon Restoration Program is helping bring falcons back from the brink of extinction after they were nearly wiped out by DDT. Birds are bred and raised in captivity and then released. Nesting boxes are placed on smokestacks and buildings to provide the high nesting places the birds prefer. 300 hatchlings were counted in 2001.

- Five days after the Michigan Senate approved a budget bill that authorized drilling beneath the lakes, the shoreline community of Grand Haven, Michigan, banned directional drilling beneath Lake Michigan. This act added to the growing controversy over directional drilling. Eight months later the Michigan Senate reversed its stand on the issue and banned drilling beneath the Great Lakes.

- State and local governments spent billions of dollars to improve wastewater treatment plants and reduce the amount of phosphorus in Lake Erie in the 1970s and 1980s. Formerly "dead" Lake Erie is now a good fishing lake.

- The United States and Canada have agreed to strive for zero discharge into the Great Lakes. This means they hope to reach a point where no pollutants are released into the environment.

WATER RESOURCES DEVELOPMENT ACT OF 1986
as amended September 2000
1962d-20. Prohibition on Great Lakes Diversions

1. The Great Lakes are the most important natural resource to the eight Great Lakes States and two Canadian provinces, providing water supply for domestic and industrial use, clean energy through hydropower production, an efficient transportation mode for moving products into and out of the Great Lakes region, and recreational uses for millions of United States and Canadian citizens;

2. The Great Lakes need to be carefully managed and protected to meet current and future needs within the Great Lakes basin and Canadian provinces...

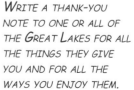

1. Read the excerpt from the Water Resources Development Act. Explain in your own words why it is important to protect the Great Lakes.

2. Both government and individuals play important roles in protecting the lakes. List ways in which government can protect the lakes. List ways individuals can protect the lakes.

3. What reasons do you think the Grand Haven City Council had for going against the State Senate and banning drilling in their community? How is this an example of democracy at work?

4. What is zero discharge? Do you think it can be achieved? Why or why not?

WRITE A THANK-YOU NOTE TO ONE OR ALL OF THE GREAT LAKES FOR ALL THE THINGS THEY GIVE YOU AND FOR ALL THE WAYS YOU ENJOY THEM.

Great Lakes Puzzlers

BOATS AND STUFF

S	L	K	Y	O	O	W	H	E	R	G	E
U	S	C	G	Z	V	H	P	S	V	R	W
R	Q	M	S	T	E	A	M	S	H	I	P
F	O	R	E	K	A	L	L	C	I	C	B
B	J	E	I	H	G	E	L	H	R	E	Y
O	K	T	E	E	P	B	L	O	B	B	Z
A	M	T	U	G	P	A	N	O	L	R	N
T	Q	U	X	P	U	C	A	N	O	E	K
N	L	C	J	E	O	K	Y	E	T	A	F
A	R	E	T	H	G	I	E	R	F	K	N
D	U	G	O	U	T	D	S	T	H	E	I
Y	O	U	B	S	E	H	C	E	E	R	B

breeches buoy
canoe
cutter
dugout
freighter
ice breaker
laker
schooner
steamship
surfboat
tug
USCG
whaleback

FISH FINDER

alewife
barbels
fins
gills
lateral line
nares
opercle
perch
scales
trout
walleye
whitefish

L	Z	B	A	R	B	E	L	S	O	A
T	A	Y	L	O	R	R	W	F	P	L
G	Q	T	X	P	E	R	C	H	P	E
I	A	R	E	E	M	V	G	S	E	W
L	N	O	C	R	M	S	N	I	F	I
L	B	U	O	C	A	U	I	F	S	F
S	W	T	J	L	P	L	W	E	E	E
A	R	S	Y	E	U	R	L	T	R	D
S	C	A	L	E	S	A	S	I	A	D
M	N	C	O	I	V	S	B	H	N	V
Q	Y	E	Y	E	L	L	A	W	F	E

BIRD WATCHER

C	E	L	G	A	E	D	L	A	B	O	P
O	A	V	E	Z	N	M	L	O	R	S	S
O	Y	N	R	E	T	T	I	B	E	O	N
T	C	Q	A	J	K	N	O	R	E	H	R
R	O	S	T	D	W	B	I	R	D	I	E
H	I	D	Y	L	A	N	C	N	L	P	T
H	E	R	R	I	N	G	G	U	L	L	K
A	S	R	E	S	O	E	O	V	I	O	C
M	A	L	L	A	R	D	E	O	K	O	A
S	R	E	P	I	P	D	N	A	S	N	L
K	I	N	G	F	I	S	H	E	R	E	B
P	I	P	I	N	G	P	L	O	V	E	R

bald eagle
bittern
black tern
Canada goose
coot
heron
herring gull
killdeer
kingfisher
loon
mallard
piping plover
sandpiper

Great Lakes Puzzlers

OUR GREAT GREAT LAKES!

DOWN

1. Water flows from one Great Lake to the next because of a change in the _____.

2. The U.S. _____ _____ is responsible for law enforcement and environmental protection on our nation's waterways.

5. Water from the Great Lakes flows into the _____ Ocean.

6. An _____ is a system formed by the relationship of organisms to their environment.

7. Early explorers like Jean _____ traveled the Great Lakes looking for water routes to Asia.

12. Ships in a channel can be raised or lowered to a different elevation by means of _____.

14. After a storm surge pushes water to one end of a lake, the water sloshing back and forth to return to normal is called a _____.

ACROSS

1. Wind and waves cause shoreline _____.

3. Acronym for the Great Lakes.

4. During the 18th century, _____ transported furs and trade goods by canoe through the Great Lakes.

8. Lake Superior is classified as _____, meaning it has fewer living organisms because of its depth and temperature.

9. Many invader species in the Great Lakes were brought from distant places in the _____ water of cargo ships.

10. A lake's moderation of temperatures and climate along the shoreline is called the lake _____.

11. The Great Lakes were formed by moving and melting _____.

13. The largest freshwater island in the world.

14. The deepest Great Lake.

15. When storm winds push lake water and raise its level at one end of the lake, it is called a _____.

16. An _____ species is a foreign plant or animal that enters an ecosystem.

USE THESE PAGES TO COMPLETE SOME OF THE IDEAS I GAVE YOU IN THE BOOK, OR USE THEM TO DRAW PICTURES, MAKE
YOUR OWN PUZZLES, OR TO MAKE A SCRAPBOOK OF POSTCARDS OR PHOTOS FROM THE GREAT LAKES.

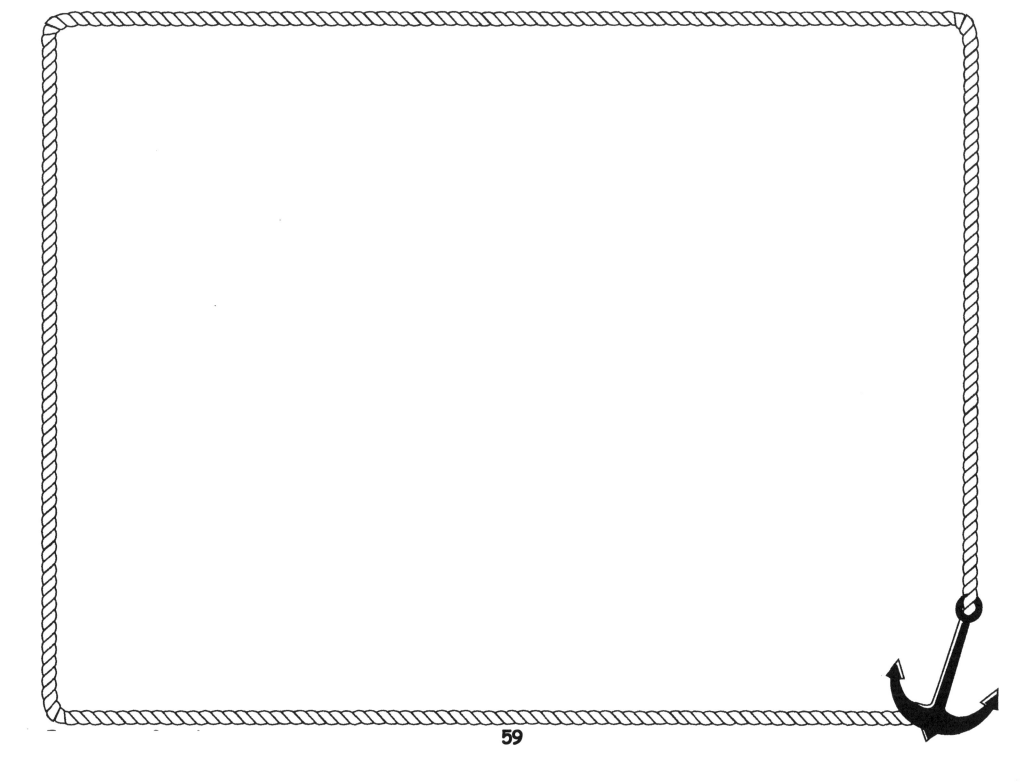

Page 4

1. C 2. C 3. C 4. C 5. A 6. C

Page 5

1. Precambrian Era. 2. Paleozoic Era. 3. volcanic activity. 4. Answers will vary but could be similiar to: The Great Lakes are very, very young compared to the ancient earth. The earth is more than 3 billion years older than the GLs. 5. Man. 6. Metals or minerals.

Page 6

1. A. Lake Michigan, A. & C. Lake Huron, A. St. Lawrence Seaway, A. Georgian Bay , A. Lake Ontario, C. Saginaw Bay, B. Lake Erie
2. Glaciers made the ancient river valleys larger and filled the valleys with water when they melted. (Answers may vary)

Page 7

1. River valleys. 2. The North Pole. 3. They compressed the earth's surface, gouged out river valleys, moved and deposited debris, changed the shape of the land, and left lakes behind. 4. They were made wider and deeper. 5. They were blocked with glacial debris. 6. Melted glaciers. Map Activity: Lake Erie.

Page 8

1. Lake Superior. 2. Lake Ontario is much deeper than Lake Erie. 3. Six (1,260 feet). 4. They are connected at the top and have similar volume, area, depth, and shape. 5. Because they hold 1/5 of the earth's fresh water supply. 6. Answers may vary.

Page 9

1. 600 feet. 2. Lake Erie and Lake Ontario, 325 feet. 3. Niagara Falls. 4. The freshwater lakes flow out into the ocean. 5. The Detroit River, Lake Erie, the Niagara River, Lake Ontario, and the St. Lawrence River. 6. T 7. T 8. F

Page 10

1. It will dry up. 2. The Atlantic Ocean because the elevation change at Niagara Falls will prevent the water from flowing into the Niagara River. 3. It might get bigger. The southwest end might flow over the land. 4. It would still flow to the Atlantic Ocean, but its water volume would decrease and the water-way would be narrower and shallower. 5. They would increase in size and water vol-ume. Skippy Question: About 50 generations. Answers may vary.

Page 11

1. Waves are energy traveling through a medium. 2. Wind. 3. Energy. 4. When a water wave approaches the shore, the bottom of the wave drags the lake bottom and the circular motion of the energy "breaks." 5. Amplitude = distance from equilibrium to the crest. 6. Crest = top of the wave. 7. Trough = bottom of the wave. 8. Wavelength = distance between crests.
Experiment: 1. The motion of the weight. 2. Up and down   3. No. 4. Wave energy. 5. The floatie is moving up and down, not forward.

Page 12

1. A seiche. 2. A surge causes a seiche. 3. Climate. 4. Levels drop because of less water entering the lakes and more evaporation. 5. Spring, because water levels are at their highest. 6. A, B, and C are all true.

Page 13

1. R 2. S 3. C   4. W
Experiment: 1. Sand. 2. Rock. 3. Lake Michigan because its shores are mainly sand and clay.   4. Lake Superior because its shores are mainly rock.

Page 14

Down: 1. Beach Pea. 2. Piping Plover. 4. Ant Lion. 5. Bearberry. *Across:* 1. Back. 2. Pond. 3. Scavenger. 6. Foredune.

Page 15

1. Purifiers. 2. Controllers. 3. Reducers. 4. Nursuries. 5. Resting. 6. Recreation.

Page 16

1. Pictured Rocks National Lakeshore. 2. Georgian Bay Islands National Park and the Door Peninsula. 3. The North Channel. 4. Door Peninsula. 5. Minerals. 6. Huron. 7. Wind and water.

Page 17

1-8. Answers will vary.

Page 18

1. Oligotrophic. 2. Cutting trees along streams warms the water, farming adds irrigation runoff of soils and fertilizers, industry adds pollutants and warm water, cities along shorelines add sewage and other pollutants. 3. It is nearing the end of its life cycle. There is little oxygen in the water to support fish. 4. land...water. 5. Lake Micihigan: oligotrophic, little life. Lake Erie: eutrophic, much life. Lake Ontario: mesotrophic, some life. Lake Huron: oligotrophic, little life. Lake Superior: olig-otrophic, little life.

Page 19

1. Nostrils. 2. Lungs. 3. Skin. 4. Arms. 5. Skeleton. 6. Hear, see, smell, and feel. A. Scales. B. Dorsal fins. C. Lateral line. D. Caudal fin. E. Eye. F. Opercle. G. Ventral fins. H. Anal fin. I. Mouth. J. Pectoral fins.

Answers

Page 21

Page 22

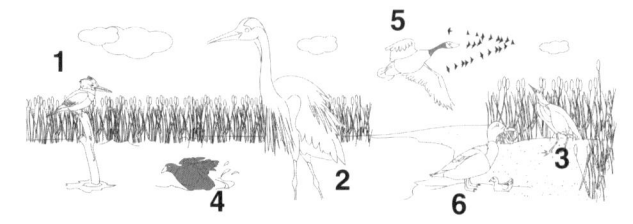

Page 23

A. 1, 4, 6.   B. 2, 3, 5. Map Activity: Sault Ste. Marie, ON; Muskegon, MI; Traverse City, MI; Cleveland, OH; Buffalo, NY.

Page 27

Claiming land & resources for France: LaSalle, Jolliet. *Building the fur trade:* Champlain, LaSalle, Duluth, Radisson & Groseilliers. *Looking for a water route to the Pacific:* Champlain, Nicolet, Brule, Marquette, Duluth, Allouez. *Bringing Christianity to the Native Americans:* Marquette, Hennepin, Allouez.

Page 29

1. $988,475.   2. $13,838,650.   3. About 7.5 miles per day.

Page 30

6 Ojibwa, 3 Iroquois, 5 Huron, 1 Neutrals, 2 Erie, 7 Menominee, 9 Miami, 4 Odawa, 8 Potawatomi.

Page 31

1. *immigrant*: a person who <u>migrates to</u> another country. *emigrant*: a person who <u>migrates from</u> another country. *mastiff*: a breed of dog. *meerschaum*: a tobacco pipe. *abode*: residence. hence: from now. *disembarking*: getting off from a boat. *mingled*: mixed together. *slain*: killed. *berths*: shelf-like sleeping space.   2. They are describing the crowded and chaotic conditions on the steamboats. Answers will vary.   3. They predict the acculturation of the immigrants, that the immigrants will assimilate into their new culture. Answers will vary.

Page 33

1. C   2. D   3. B   4. C   5. A   6. A
7. C   8. D   9. A   10. C

Page 34

From top to bottom: #1 dugout canoe, #4 schooner, #2 bark canoe, #6 whaleback, #5 steamship, #3 square-rigged sailing ship, #7 freighter.

Page 35

Fishery, Pollution, alewife, hatchery. Answer: Yellow Perch.

Page 36

1. A steep change in elevation. 2. about 115 degrees. 3. There is a shipwreck above the water NE of Squaw Island. There is a sunken wreck NW of Garden Island. There is a wreck east of Garden Island marked *Wreck 5*. It is 5 feet below the surface. 4. Soundings are the numbers on the map. They indicate water depth. A skipper uses them to make sure her boat won't run aground. 5. There are three "Red Nun" buoys and one "Green Can" buoy. (The "G Fl 4s" marker on the east end of Garden Island Shoal is a buoy that flashes a green light for four seconds.) 6. There is a swampy area on the east side of Garden Island. 7. Rocky areas are marked *rky* or with asterisks in many locations; east of Garden Island there are many. *Tricky Trip:* The captain will be anchoring over a power cable, and will run aground where the depth is two feet.

Page 39

The Coast Guard's responsibilities include national security, environmental protection, search and rescue, boater safety, icebreaking, and buoy tending. A breeches buoy was a rescue device used from the 1840s through the 1950s to remove people from stranded ships. Its name comes from its breeches-like design. Buoys direct boat traffic, mark hazards, sometimes collect weather data, and sometimes measure wave height and other surface conditions. Great Lakes shipping hazards include rocky shores, storms, and fog. The Coast Guard saves approximately 4,000 lives each year.

Page 40

1. 1,167 trucks. 2. 583 rail cars. 3. US-built and -crewed ships are all subject to the same standards, regulations, and inspections to ensure safe construction and operation. Answers will vary.

Page 41

A. Ocean Bulk Freighter. B. Self-Unloading Laker. C. Lakes Bulk Freighter. D. Ocean General Cargo Vessel.

Page 42

1. Answers will vary. A code is an invented communication system that uses symbols (letters, shapes, sounds, etc.) to represent language. 2. Answers will vary. Natural languages are not invented, they have native speakers. Languages represent meaning directly, whereas codes represent languages.

Answers

Page 43

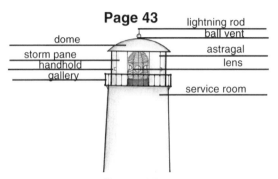

dome, lightning rod, ball vent, storm pane, astragal, handhold, lens, gallery, service room

Page 44

1. They link the Great Lakes into a "water highway" that stretches from Lake Superior to the Atlantic Ocean. This encouraged 19th-century expansion and growth in the midwest and makes commercial shipping possible today. 2. Because canals were being built that allowed settlers to travel by water easier than by land. 3. Because people traveled and traded along water routes before roads were cleared in the forested interior.

Page 45

1. Your height minus four feet. 2. Aqueduct: a structure like a bridge that carries water over a valley. Answers will vary. 3. Answers will vary; the canal was 363 miles long.

Page 46

4, 1, 3, 5, 2.

Page 47

1. 552 divided by room height. 2. 3,800 divided by room length; about 12 and a half football fields. 3. Answers will vary.

Page 48

1. T 2. B 3. T 4. B 5. N 6. B 7. B 8. B 9. T 10. N 11. B 12. N 13. N 14. T 15. N

Page 49

1-7 Answers will vary. 8. Restaurants, ice cream stands, gift shops, golf courses, gas stations, hotels & motels, fruit farms, museums, grocery stores.

Page 50

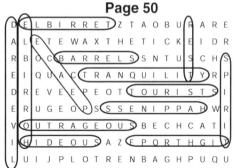

answers to clues: 1. horrible, terrible, hideous, outrageous. 2. tourists. 3. daredevil. 4. barrel, tightrope. 5. tranquility, happiness, rest, peace. 6. spirit.

Page 51

1. Three small fish. The larger fish, which is higher in the food chain, contains more toxins (biomagnification). 2. bioaccumulation. 3. biomagnification. 4. birth defects/thin egg shells, cancer, death. Falcon egg shells were too thin and broke during development, depleting the falcon population. 5. A fish-eating bird contains 50 times more DDT than a small fish.

Page 52

1. The drop in the fish population due to the sea lamprey ended commercial fishing there in the 1940s. 2. 14,700,000 pounds per year. 3. Answers will vary, but may include: the sea lamprey and other invader species; people who alter the waterways; commercial shipping that brings ocean species into the lakes. 4. Answers will vary, but may include restaurants, grocery stores, sport fishing, tourism. *Organize the Info:* 1. Atlantic Ocean. 2. The Welland Canal was altered, allowing them to bypass Niagara Falls. 3. Depleted fish populations hurt commercial fishing. 4. Joint U.S. and Canadian efforts, including TFM, and limiting reproduction.

Page 53

1. Filter feeding. 2. Too many plants grow in the filtered water. 3. Small fish can't get enough plankton to eat and die; sport fish eat the highly contaminated zebra mussels. 4. Colonies of zebra mussels can clog water intakes, damage boat motors, sink buoys, and are a nuisance on the beach. They also make drinking water taste bad and contaminate sport fish. 5. Sport fish eat zebra mussels, which, through filter feeding, accumulate large amounts of toxins.

Page 54

1. Slant drilling. 2. Sale of Great Lakes water. 3. Because the two countries share the Great Lakes and its resources and are equally affected by changes in the lakes. 4. To protect the water of the Great Lakes; without it people could sell Great Lakes water, possibly reducing water levels and altering the ecosystem. 5. Answers will vary but may include: difficulty of foreseeing problems; it has never been done before; even though it seems safe, the damage caused by one accident would be too great. 6. Answers will vary.

Page 55

1. Answers will vary but may include: the Great Lakes are an important resource because they provide water for homes and industry, transportation, recreation, and power generation. 2. Answers may include the following. *Government:* passing laws that

Answers

protect the lakes from pollution, exploitation of resources, and destruction of ecosystems. *Individuals:* not polluting the water and beaches, not spreading invader species, and staying informed about issues that affect the lakes.   3. Answers may include: the City Council wanted to take a stand against slant drilling and make it an issue of public concern, or they wanted to avoid destruction of beach habitat, possible damage to the lake ecosystem, reduction of lake levels, and unwanted drilling sites in the community. This illustrates the core democratic values of popular sovereignty (that people make decisions with their votes) and the common good (that we have a duty to work together to improve our community and country). 4. No pollutants being released into the environment. Answers will vary.

Boats and Stuff

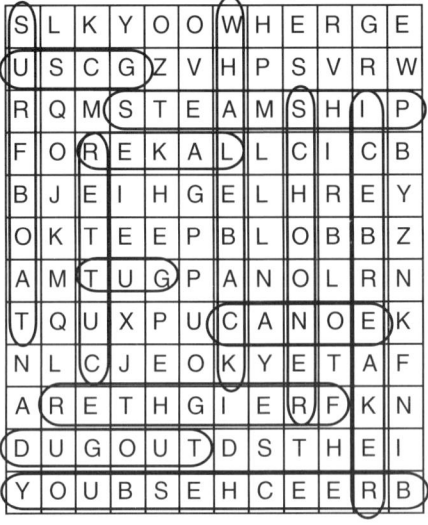

Fish Finder

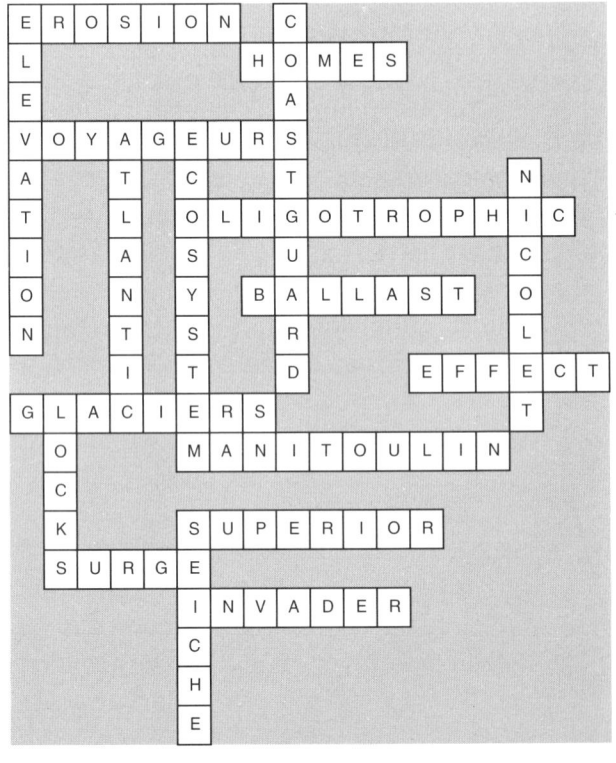

Bird Watcher

Our Great Great Lakes!